The Golden Light of a Spiritual Dawn

The Golden Light of a Spiritual Dawn

Blair T. Atherton

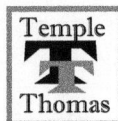

Temple
T
Thomas

Cover design by Tobi Afran

Published by Temple Thomas Publishing
Coral Springs, FL.

ISBN: 979-8-218-10247-0

This book is dedicated to all who search for meaning and purpose and seek greater spiritual awareness and understanding.

Contents

Preface

This book is an anthology of selected articles from my blog site, *Exploring Spirituality Beyond Religion.* Selections span the period from 2013-2022. I decided to publish the collection in print because the book will far out live the web site.

The format is that of a spiritual diary. It traces the evolution of my understanding of spirituality at the most fundamental level. The book identifies the spiritual attributes and behaviors needed to reach higher levels of spiritual awareness.

There were times when I was compelled to stop what I was doing and start writing. When the urge to write and inspiration were strongest, the words flowed onto the page without thinking about what I was writing. These are my most prized entries because the messages they convey are the most compelling.

It is my hope that the spiritual wisdom found in this book will be shared and distributed as widely as possible. I pray that the spiritual truths published here will be found by all of those who are ready to hear them.

The spirit Silver Birch has said many times that if we can help but one person to rise up out of darkness, defeat, or despair, or help one person who is lost and searching for meaning, then our life has been worth living. I hope that this book will succeed in this.

Acknowledgements

I would like to express my gratititude to everyone who, over the last nine years, chose to explore articles found on my Wordpress blog site, *Explorig Spirituality Beyond Religion.* Your interest and open mindedness fueled my desire to keep writing.

I want to thank Tobi Afran for her wonderful work in designing the cover of this book. She took my vision concerning mood, the colors I wanted included, along with elements of the book title, and created an evocative and truly extraordinary design.

Over the last decade, I delved into a variety of scripture and other spiritual writings, such as the Hindu *Upanishads,* the teachings of Buddha, the *Old* and *New Testaments,* the *Gnostic Gospels, the Qur'an,* and the series of books that are a compilation of the teachings of Silver Birch, among others. I'm grateful for the spiritual wisdom each of these sources has contributed to my broader spiritual understanding.

Prelude

I awoke in the golden light of my spiritual dawn.
The warm glow of unconditional love enveloped me

Like a mother's warmth after a baby's delivery
from womb, nurturing and reassuring.

I was compelled to set out on a pilgrimage in search of
greater spiritual awareness and understanding.

The journey has been transformative.

I am no longer who I once was,
But not yet who I, and humanity, are destined to be.

...Come, walk with me.

May 19, 2013

A Word about Religion

The Virtues of Quiet Devotion and the Prehistoric Mind

Man has taken the basic concepts of spirituality and created dogmatic and rigid religious institutions. While we may call for freedom of religion, we overlook the fact that there is often little freedom allowed *within* some organized religions. Too many people blindly follow the attitudes and edicts of their religion and religious leaders without first applying their God-given reason.

We commonly associate the worship of God with established religions. However, there are many ways to worship God within a religious dogma, or external to organized religion all together. I am in favor of a quiet devotion to God without the limitations and distractions of rituals.

I believe that quiet devotion to God can be the deepest, truest, and most profound kind of relationship you can have with Him. I believe this to be so, in part because you are not seeking any sort of recognition from your fellow man for your piety. It is a pure and intimate relationship with God, unfettered by appearances and rituals.

There are many out there who share this concept of quiet, unpretentious worship. But their devotion to God is unseen by others except perhaps through their compassionate, gentle, and caring ways. I share with you what follows to illustrate that there are other ways to worship God than through the rituals and traditions of organized religion.

At the same time, many religious teachings have great value by providing a moral code for how we should live our lives. It is the intolerance and fanaticism of some "religious" people that I find objectionable.

Many of us have been indoctrinated by our religion leading us to believe it is the only (right) way to show devotion to God. There are myriad ways to give homage to God, and not all involve affiliation with a particular religion. It is not for us to say which practice is better than another. A person's relationship with God is a very personal one, and should not be subject to scrutiny or criticism by others.

At the same time, one should not try to impose their religious beliefs and attitudes on others. To attempt to do so, in effect, is a dismissal of other valid means of worship.

This leads us to the notion (in some, but not all religions or members) that the people of one religion or another are the "chosen people" of God, or that there is only one "right" way to worship God.

The concept of a chosen people has always baffled me as it does not stand to reason and it defies logic. God created all people and loves all of His children. Why would He favor one group over another? A mother does not give birth to two children only to love one and despise the other. She gave them life. She loves them both even though they may have different personalities and pursue different paths in life. She tries to guide both and help them find their way, but in the end they will each choose their own path.

Is one way to worship God better than another? In my view, God does not require or expect elaborate rituals or traditions. These are practices were created by man. I believe that we should at least acknowledge His existence and give thanks for the many gifts and blessings He gives to all of us. These are the essence of "worship." In this minimalist view, little more is required.

If you wish to offer morning and evening prayers, go to mass on Sundays, burn incense in front of the Buddha, or pray to the Great Spirit in the Sky, so be it. No one way is better than another, or more pleasing to God's eye than another. They are all expressions of devotion to God.

Where things go wrong is when people try to impose their religion on others, or judge others in the context of their religious beliefs.

What are the most basic, fundamental aspects of a belief in God and what are their implications? One way to approach this question is to try to imagine you have gone back to prehistoric times before there was any religion. Imagine you have become aware that there must be a creator or something greater than yourself. How does that affect your outlook on life?

Here are some ideas that came into my prehistoric mind.

- Belief in God means that we acknowledge His existence.
- Acknowledging His existence suggests that we should communicate with Him in some way.
- Knowing that He is watching suggests that we should maintain a sense of accountability for our actions and how we treat others.
- All of the inhabitants of the earth came from Him and are a part of Him. Therefore, we should cherish and respect all life on earth.
- Awe and wonder about the magnitude and mysteries of the universe give homage to God's greatness and acknowledges our diminutive existence in the expanse of creation.

As a civilization, we have become perhaps too dogmatic in our view of religion and worship. The ideas above illustrate how simple the conceptual framework surrounding spirituality and a belief in God can be.

May 25, 2013

Spirituality as a State of Being.

Spirituality does not reside in flowery talk of love, light, or communion with angels and spirit guides. In fact, spirituality is a very serious and deep subject that needs to be understood because it is an integral, critical part of our existence. Not everyone expresses their spirituality and consequently is unable to live a truly happy, fulfilled life.

I believe that spirituality is a state of being and a way of living. It is an expression of the spirit-self in everyday life. It is the certainty of the presence of God in us and all of creation. It is recognition of our divine self as a part of our creator. It is the realization that we are an integral part of the Source, not a disassociated remnant or emanation from it. This knowledge brings with it great responsibility.

The fact that we can exist in physical and spirit form at the same time may seem a contradiction. What is not understood by many is that our true existence is one of spirit. The body is like a garment the spirit wears for a short time that will be shed when it is no longer needed. It is a means by which we materialize in the physical world to engage in learning and attend to our life lessons.

But in putting on the garment, many things are hidden from us. We may lose sight of the spirit beneath the clothing. We may lose touch with our divinity hidden behind the shroud of our physicality. Looking in from the outside, we strain to see the bits of light that penetrate the fabric. Oftentimes, all we can see is waves of subdued light and shadows of what is inside. Our spirituality lies there beckoning us like a distant memory we struggle to recall.

Spirituality is a state of being, knowing, and living. It is expressed and characterized through our actions, not our words. It is an expansion of consciousness that sees beyond the body and the self. It is awareness that all things are a part of God and deserving of our love and respect.

If we are integral to God, then we have the qualities and potential for infinite love. This means we are imbued with the qualities of love and compassion for all living things. These are at the core of our divine nature, and spirituality cannot exist without their expression.

Thus, to understand and express our spirituality, we must find a way to express our divine nature in our everyday lives through our actions and how we live our lives.

June 1, 2013

The Light Inside of You

In the last entry, I used the imagery of the body as a garment within which lay the spirit. Here I would like to share with you a verse I wrote a long time ago and that

appears in my first book that likens our spirituality to rays
of light that we too often shut away. And having done so, it
continually strains for release.

For only a few fleeting moments
Have I felt the warm light of you
Of what is inside of you.

Those moments were like rays of light
Peeking through the cracks of a door
In a dark room.

I am in the darkness alone,
Longing to know
What lies on the other side of the door.
Yearning to feel the touch
Of the warm and beautiful
Light that lies there.

But the door is locked,
The key to its opening
Unknown to me.
So I will wait—
Yes, wait patiently
For the next beam of light
To spill through the cracks.
Longing to know

To understand
To embrace
The wonderful light
That shines inside of you.

June 8, 2013

To What Doth My Heart Hearken?

To what doth my heart hearken?

This is the question that haunts me in every waking moment.

Though it beats in my chest, my heart seems somehow abstract and transcendent.

It calls to me with sweet refrain.

And like the Siren my heart's song draws me in a new direction.

But not to destruction; rather, to new meaning and purpose.

I do not want to resist; the melody is too beautiful.

The notes hit a chord that makes my spirit sing.

I am compelled to seek the source of this wondrous beauty, so that I may come to know it in its fullness.

What would you have me do I ask?

The answer came swiftly and powerfully in a single word

That echoed and resonated in the essence of my being—
LOVE!

June 22, 2013

What is Love?

It is easy to get confused concerning which feelings are love and which are not. The problem may come from what we refer to as physical attraction. The attraction may be sexual (e.g., they are good-looking or good in bed), or psychological (e.g., the forbidden fruit, one's celebrity, wealth or position, or the classic "bad boy" [or girl] attraction). These are all based on physical elements.

Likely, we have all seen high failure rates for relationships that arose from these factors. This suggests that there is a lot of confusion out there concerning the physical versus the transcendent aspects of love. The physical motivators for "love" are consistent with the materialistic values that seem to be so widespread today.

It is uncertain to what degree the transcendent quality of love is experienced by lovers today given the high divorce rate. Could true love be an expression of the spirit that transcends the body and all physical modalities? Could true love for another be a *spirit(ual)* attraction and experience?

There are different contexts in which we love another—that between a parent and child, between friends, romantic love between lovers, and so forth. Societal norms dictate limits on how we can *physically* express love in these various types of relationships. However, I believe that love is love regardless of the context. That is, I do not believe that transcendent love varies by context, only how it is physically expressed.

I believe that love is a form of spiritual energy that is independent of biology and worldly context. Love as spiritual energy may be heralded by that sense of a mutual connection between people. It is a spiritual connection not a physical one. This is what we look for in a mate and find in our family and best friends. When will we learn to go beyond the physical and start to listen to what our spirit tells us?

July 6, 2013

Spirituality: A Life of Action

There are many attributes with which one can compare people. This is a murky business because things are rarely just black and white. It is more a question of which human attributes are more prominent than others in an individual.

When it comes to exhibiting spirituality, it seems there are those who primarily talk and think about it, and others who mainly do things to help others.

Both are important and contribute to our understanding of what it means to be a spiritual person. However, I believe that one's actions are far more important in defining one's spirituality than simply talking about it. Spirituality is a way of living rather than a way of thinking or talking.

It may seem odd to say that actions such as going to one's place of worship regularly, or reading the scriptures may or may not be indicators of a truly spiritual person. Some of you may know people who do these things, but whose behavior otherwise militate against their being spiritual.

I believe that love and compassion for others are the foundation for living a spiritual life, or as I prefer to say, living the life of spirit. But not as a concept; rather, love and compassion are an expressions or outlets for our spirituality. I believe these two attributes to be at the core of our divinity. If someone is unable, for whatever reason, to express these two attributes, then the path to expression of their spirit-self probably has not yet begun.

More likely is that we do not consistently exhibit love and compassion. We may have biases or prejudices through which we filter who is "deserving" of our love and compassion. This is wherein lies the challenge in trying to fully express our spirit. As hard as it may be, we should strive to have love and compassion for *everyone*.

It might help to remind ourselves that we do not know what demons others face in life. We do not know what experiences have shaped their current state of existence. We do not know the nature of the karma that brought them to where they are.

But whatever these unknowns may be, we need to try our best to give them the benefit of the doubt and extend a helping hand whenever we can, even though sometimes they might slap it away.

July 13, 2013

Wherefrom Comes Happiness?

In this day and age, we live in a world that focuses on, and values, material things rather than the spiritual qualities of existence. This has led to the widespread rise of the ignoble qualities of personality in many people such as pride, ego, greed, selfishness, narcissism, and self-aggrandizement. Sadly, it appears that a surprising number of people have not known any other way to live.

At the same time, many of these same people are realizing that success in their career, prestige, and the accumulation of worldly possessions does not bring the happiness they assumed would follow. This has been demonstrated to us again and again through people we know and from stories of celebrities we read about or see on TV. We shake our heads and ask why happiness has eluded such privileged people.

What I have come to know in reflecting on my life is that material things did not make me happy. Rather, loving and helping others has brought me the greatest happiness, satisfaction, and fulfillment.

Although worldly possessions will not bring happiness, wanting for things you do not have can make you _un_happy. It is the wanting itself that brings discontent, not the lack of things desired.

In my view, we should not be asking God for material things. God gives each of us the gifts and material things that he wishes us to have and that best serve our life plan. We should accept these with genuine gratitude and give thanks. Rather than ask for more, we should share what we have with others, especially the less fortunate.

I believe that praying should be reserved for giving thanks for what God has given to us, no matter how meager it may seem, and to ask for help for ourselves or others who are sick, in pain, or who are having difficulty with the trials and tribulations of everyday life. When we focus on others, the "need," desire, and wanting for materials things disappears, and our spirit begins to express itself.

We need to find a way to replace wanting with unselfish giving. It's not complicated. This truly is the key to happiness and a spiritual way of life.

July 20, 2013

An insidious Intruder

Trying to eliminate ego has been kind of like a teeter-totter for me; just when I think I have it squashed, it pops up again out of nowhere. Over time, I have managed to reduce it to a weak and sickly thing that has only brief rallies of influence before it is sent back to bed.

I have been working to rid myself of ego for many years. It's a work in progress that I find quite liberating. It requires a lot of conscious effort and determination to extinguish ego, or more accurately to keep it at bay.

By ego I mean a need for recognition, excessive pride, and a feeling of superiority to others. I believe that the prevalence of ego in today's society is a consequence of materialistic values that appear to be the guiding principle of the majority these days.

As a young man, prior to embarking on my career, I was very humble and all about self-sacrifice and helping others. However, I remember an incident later in life that happened at a time when I was enjoying great success in my career. It illustrates how ego can unwittingly overshadow one's spirituality and disengage one from compassion.

I was walking down a city street with my son when he was 12 or 13 years old. We came upon a homeless man walking toward us. The man was dirty, in rags, weak and trembling. When we met, he did not speak but put his hand out for alms. I ignored him and shuffled my boy past.

My son stopped and grabbed my arm surprised at my lack of compassion. He insisted that I give him some money for the man, and he straight away gave it to him. I had no idea what I had become until that moment.

It is difficult for me to admit to having had such a failure of character. I attribute it to ego as it happened during a time, I realize in retrospect, when my ego had a strong hold on me. The innocence and generosity of a child had shown me the depravity of spirit that existed in me during that period of my life. It took a while, but thankfully, I managed to crawl out of the muck of ego, put on clean clothes, and reclaim my spirituality.

This taught me that ego is insidious; it gradually invades the psyche little by little so that one does not notice that it is happening. It can slowly become a more and more prominent part of one's personality and behavior. By the time your ego is full grown, you are not even aware of what a selfish and self-serving lump you have become.

Ego and the materialistic way of life go hand-in-hand. An inflated image of oneself is intimately intertwined with the selfishness, greed, and lack of compassion we see today.

This is because ego is one of the motivators that drive us to try to seek recognition and prestige from the things we have, where we live, and those with whom we associate.

I may be sticking my neck out here, but I do not think that recognition and prestige are basic human needs. I believe they are *created* needs from very effective marketing strategies that span decades. So many advertisements we see play to, or seek to create in us, a "need" for prestige or just being noticed whether it is for white teeth, a flashy car, a big house, or expensive clothes. We must find a way to resist and reclaim our humility and dignity.

How does ego conflict with becoming a more spiritual person? The egotist's primary concern is *their* needs. Consequently, ego can prevent us from seeing what those around us need. The sense of superiority that comes with ego can cause us to dismiss or overlook the adversity, suffering, and deprivation that others endure. This is one of the main ways that ego compromises expression of our spirit and militates against our becoming a spiritual person.

We are not defined or valued as individuals or human beings by what we have, how we look, or who our friends are. We are defined by the degree of humility we exhibit, how we live our lives, and how we treat other people; these are indicators of the degree to which we have become a spiritual person.

July 27, 2013

Shall the Meek Inherit the Earth?

Those of you with Christian backgrounds may recall the Beatitudes presented by Jesus during his Sermon on the Mount. They are all wonderful sayings by which to live a spiritual life.

One of my favorites is "Blessed are the meek for they shall inherit the earth." This beatitude has been interpreted from the original Greek in a number of slightly different ways. For example, "Earth" has also been interpreted to mean the Kingdom of Heaven which gives the Beatitude a decidedly spiritual meaning. Alternate translations of the word "meek" include humble, gentle, and poor.

This beatitude could be interpreted as prophesy of things to come, or simply as a statement of the most desirable sort of spiritual (and human) disposition. I favor the latter possibility. Although, I suppose, it is possible that all of the power hungry egotists could end up wiping each other out, leaving us "meek," but not weak, spiritual people to transform humanity and save the earth.

I see meek or humble people as having great strength, self-confidence, and restraint. They have a certainty that they are on the right path regardless of what others may think. Humble people understand that any talents they may have are gifts from God, and as such, credit should be given to Him whenever they are applied with good effect.

I believe that we should add humility and gentleness to our list of characteristics that describe spiritual persons. Who would be better than the "meek" to make the Kingdom of Heaven a reality on Earth?

August 2, 2013

"All that is composed shall be decomposed."

In the traditional or canonical gospels found in the *New Testament* of the *Bible*, Jesus gives us a wonderful way of looking at spirituality and how to live a truly spiritual life. There are other records of the teachings of Jesus that were excluded from the *New Testament*. They are referred to collectively as the Gnostic Gospels. I found three: *The Gospel of Phillip, The Gospel of Thomas, and the Gospel of Mary Magdalene.*

After reading all three, the first thing that struck me was that they were almost completely devoid of stories about miracles. Instead they were composed of what we might call the wisdom or sayings of Jesus. I saw nothing heretical about them; rather, they provided additional teachings to compliment those in the *New Testament.* The three gospels provided a great deal of food for thought concerning spirituality.

That is especially true for the *Gospel of Mary Magdalene.* It was frustrating to learn that ten of the pages are missing. Frustrating because the missing pages are adjacent to what I feel are some of the most mysterious passages. What happened to the missing pages? Were they removed by someone to withhold certain secrets of spirituality, or simply damaged or lost? What do we *not* know in their absence?

The first ten lines from the *Gospel of Mary Magdalene* that follow had an especially powerful effect on me. The six pages that preceded these passages are missing from the documents that were found.

[...] "What is matter?

Will it last forever?"

The Teacher answered:

"All that is born, all that is created,

20

All the elements of nature are interwoven and united with each other.

All that is composed shall be decomposed;

Everything returns to its roots;

Matter returns to the origins of matter.

Those who have ears let them hear."

The basic ideas in these passages are not new to me, but my reaction to them was totally unexpected. When I read these lines in the gospel, it felt like primal memories buried deep in my soul came crashing forward revealing a fundamental, profound truth. The feelings were so powerful that I felt a little disoriented and confused.

These passages spoke to me on a very deep level. The words were both mysterious and wonderful. All of creation is interwoven and united—yes! All that is composed shall be decomposed—that is, all that is physical is transitory. Everything shall return to the source.

We are drawn to the source of all creation. It is a force of nature that transcends belief. It is that inexplicable yearning for meaning and purpose unique to the human condition. It is the search for our spirit-self and its birthplace.

August 17, 2013

Nature: A More Expansive Spirituality

When we go to beautiful wild places to get away from it all, it is sometimes difficult to describe what we feel. For me, it is an inexplicable feeling of a belonging—a homecoming of sorts. It is a joyful feeling like I have met my soul mate. I want to linger endlessly and I lament when I must return to the steel and cement world.

This feeling of nature—the trees, animals, bugs, rocks, etc. as soul mate says something very profound. For those few hours, days, or however long in beautiful natural surroundings, we are on the threshold of awareness that we are a part of all of the earth and all living things that comprise nature. They are all a part of God and his divinity is a part of us and all things. As Jesus has told us in the *Gospel of Mary Magdalene*, "All that is born, all that is created, all the elements of nature are interwoven and united with each other."

Recognition of this truth has implications. One is that we are participating in an evolution of all life on Earth. We are but one species among many on a trajectory of growth in consciousness and spiritual awareness. This knowledge carries with it great responsibility. If all things are a part of God, then all things are sacred and demand our reverence, respect, compassion, and protection.

Although we may see humanity as superior to other forms of life, God may not share such an egocentric view. If that is the case, then other species may hold potential for development equal to us in God's eyes. It could be that they are just not as far along in their evolution as we.

Thomas Berry believed that God placed humanity *within* the natural order rather than above it. It is our arrogance as a species that sees itself as the one most pleasing in the eyes of God. Given the direction that humanity has taken in recent history, this may not be the case.

If God is everywhere and in all things, then exploitation and destruction of our planet and the life it holds are affronts to God. It is our arrogance in believing that our science and technology can master the forces of nature or improve on what God has created that has led to our current environmental, social, and spiritual crisis.

At the same time, I see a quiet, unobtrusive movement in progress. I see more and more people exhibiting various levels of spiritual enlightenment concerning the environment. I see small steps that help to reduce harm to the planet like buying organically grown foods, moving away from a meat-centered diet toward a more vegetarian diet, avoiding genetically modified food products (GMOs), greater sensitivity to animal rights, recycling, driving hybrid or electric cars, and so forth.

While these may seem like small things, they suggest a growing awareness of what has been discussed here. They are indications of the beginning of a step forward in spiritual evolution and awareness that will change the world in so many wonderful ways.

August 28, 2013

An Impediment to Spiritual Progression

Nature is an all pervasive spirit of love and beauty that fills and nurtures all things. All living things are her offspring and each is loved equally by her. So too, all of her children should love one another to the same degree and without prejudice or favoritism.

Last week's entry on spirituality and nature raises issues about how we view and treat animals. These matters derive in part from the statement "If all things are a part of God, then all things are sacred and demand our reverence, respect, compassion, and protection."

I believe that animals are at a higher level of consciousness than we may think. Each has its place and role in the spiritual ecology of our world. Animals have as much right to life and freedom as we.

As noted last week, it is our arrogance and self-serving nature that leads us to view animals as inferior and/or as food items put here for our consumption. I believe deep inside of me that it is wrong to raise animals for food. For me, it is a fundamental spiritual truth that compelled me to become a vegetarian.

Like any wrong, raising animals in large numbers for food has consequences. Negative impacts on the environment like pollution and global warming are a few examples of the consequential damages of the meat industry. There is also a huge toll on the spiritual progression of those who eat meat, support the farming of animals for food, or otherwise refuse to believe that animal life is as precious as human life.

Animals raised for food must endure a great deal of pain and suffering inflicted by the cultivation and slaughter process. Generally, we don't want to know much about how livestock are treated and slaughtered because we don't want to feel guilty about consuming meat. We know it is wrong, but we do not want to give up our favorite foods. We have come to love the smell of burning flesh and the taste of blood. Would you give up meat if it would save the planet, or if it would remove a major impediment to your reaching new heights of spiritual awareness?

We try to rationalize our choice by saying that if we give up all meat, it will have no measurable effect on the meat industry or the environment. We tell ourselves that one person cannot change the world.

But this misses the point. The world is changed by one person at a time doing what is right without regard to what others think or do. As more and more people act on their conscience, the next thing you know, changes can be seen, and over time the world is transformed.

One may argue that man has been killing animals for food since time immemorial. But man also has an equally long history of brutality and little regard for human life as well. However, through the ages, humanity as a whole has progressed in its spiritual evolution and now the brutality and large scale killing of humans is primarily reduced to relatively small groups of religious extremists and dictatorial fanatic groups.

As a race, our spiritual awareness has reached the point where we have come to understand that killing each other is wrong. The next step in our spiritual evolution is to recognize that killing animals is wrong.

September 4, 2013

A Spiritual Lifestyle

This blog has discussed what it means to be a spiritual person from a variety of perspectives. From what has been covered so far, we can begin to see the attributes of a spiritual lifestyle.

How many of us have the fortitude, commitment, and determination to actually *live* a spiritual life? It would seem that much of the world is headed in the opposite direction. There is immense pressure for us to conform to the materialistic, self-serving, and ego driven ways of the majority. Truly spiritual people are oftentimes unseen, sometimes down trodden, and seemingly left behind in today's fast-paced, narcissistic society.

However, in reality, it is the materialists who are being left behind. Society fosters the attitude of "live for today" without regard for the consequences of our actions for tomorrow, for the karma of this, or our next lifetime, and especially for one's spiritual development and progression.

We are all caught up in this windstorm of materialism to varying degrees. It is all around us, and it has shaped the values of a declining society. It seems a great many people do not know any other way to live.

The disillusionment and distrust with organized religion has certainly not helped. It has resulted in not only a self-imposed excommunication from religion, but also from many of the moral and scared values embedded in religious teachings. I hope that those who have left their religion have not also abandoned a belief in God.

A major theme in my writing and in my beliefs is that the most important thing whether you participate in organized religion or not is to live a life of goodness, moderation, compassion, humility, and charity. What matters most is how we treat other people. To a great extent this is what defines us as individuals and as a society.

October 2, 2013

Harmony between Spirit, Mind, and Body

It seems to me that one of the goals as a spiritual person is to achieve harmony between the spirit, mind, and body.

Here, I would define harmony as congruity between these three aspects of being. All three are integral parts of our existence, and as such interact with, and influence one another.

I think congruity is a key word here. In order for there to be harmony, the mind must be aware of the spirit and understand the nature, meaning, and purpose of a spiritual life. The mind must also be committed to a life of goodness and virtue. The body finds congruity by cultivating good health to fully support expression of the mind and spirit through outward action.

The state of the mind determines the extent to which the spirit is able to express itself. If the mind is at peace, open, and seeks spiritual awareness, it will come. When this happens, the mind is compelled to seek outlets for expression of the spirit-self. There is a transformation in one's motives, intent, and desire.

When harmony is achieved, love and compassion for all things dominates the person's world view. One's thoughts are outwardly directed toward the needs of others. There is a strong desire to serve God and humanity, and material things become relatively unimportant. Expression of the spirit energizes mind and body bringing feelings of happiness and well-being.

Prayer for Harmony

Dear God,

I strive to make myself whole, and by doing so come closer to you.

I wish to find the sacred harmony between spirit, mind, and body.

My only desire is to serve and honor you by expression of my spirit through acts of love and compassion.

I pray that my spirit may one day become attuned with, and radiate your divine love for all things. Amen

Comment

It is well known that if you are stressed or depressed, the body responds with changes in its physiological state. There may be changes in blood pressure and suppression of the immune system that make the body more susceptible to illness.

I believe that the body naturally knows what it needs to do to achieve and maintain a state of perfect health, but too often we override our natural mechanisms for balance and health through overreaction to things that happen to us, and engaging in poor eating habits.

The mind must become aware of the spirit-self to facilitate their interaction. Once the mind is aware of the spirit-self, then the spirit can begin to express itself. Those who are pure of heart and whose spiritual development has progressed to sufficiently high levels may be allowed to express spiritual gifts such as healing and mediumship. But such persons are only a tiny percentage of the world population and tend to quietly and unobtrusively carry out their spiritual work.

October 16, 2013

The Night is Too Long

What goes through the mind of someone who is dying slowly over weeks, months, or years of a disease like cancer? We try to imagine what they think about, but we can't really. We try to find things to talk about to take their mind off of the pain, sorrow, and anxiety, but we can't be sure they are listening.

What goes through a person's mind when they know they will not get better, but instead only weaker? What goes through someone's mind when they realize that their independence is gone and they can never go home again? What goes through a person's mind when they know they must leave their loved ones behind not knowing if they will ever see them again?

We do our best to make them comfortable, bring them foods they like, and celebrate their lives through old family photos. They may cry in response to old familiar songs that elicit a host of fond memories of the past. We try to tell them that they should be happy and thankful for these things remembered. Still they grieve for days gone by that cannot be relived. They lament the empty days ahead in a life fading away slowly and methodically.

We see their jaw and lips quiver as they reach for a bite of food. Their hands shake as they reach for their glass. We struggle to conceal our sorrow in seeing someone who was so strong and steady, now so tentative and frail. We try to be strong but sometimes after we've gone home, the night is too long and we break down. But that doesn't matter because the night is always too long for them.

We want very much to somehow ease their transition, but we don't know how. So we go back to be with them the next day and the next in the hope that our presence will somehow make them feel better and less anxious. All we can really do is let them know how much we love them. What is going through their minds? We try to imagine, but we can't. The night is too long.

October 24, 2013

Affirmations for Enhancing Spirituality

How can we enhance our spiritual way of living? There are a number of ways, but I would like to discuss something called affirmations. These can be very effective in changing things about ourselves and also to enhance behaviors that contribute to our fulfillment as a spiritual person.

I was first introduced to this practice by a book titled *Creative Visualization* by Shakti Gawain. Her focus was mainly on enhancing one's material life. For my own part, I have used affirmations primarily for changes in behavior, and enhancement of a spiritual way of living.

The idea is that you send out requests into the universe (or to the subconscious mind or to the higher self depending how you wish to view it). Once the request has been floated, the universe goes to work to make it happen. It is important that you do not have any preconceived notions about how the request should or will be fulfilled. Further, affirmations must be positive statements about a new state desired, not statements about what you do *not* want to be.

An affirmation is the assertion that something (*already*) exists or is true. The idea is that if you repeat something over and over with conviction and total confidence that it already exists, then it eventually will come to be.

However, the change will not happen immediately; it takes time for transformation to occur. You must be patient and consistent in making your affirmations. A good practice is to identify a time to do your affirmations at least once a day. For example, I often do them when I take a walk and/or during my daily Tai Chi practice. But you should do them whenever you think of it throughout the day. You can work on them one at a time, or several together, but not more than two or three in a given session. Too many at a time weakens the power of each individual request.

Affirmations can also be done as a sort of meditation where you focus intently on what you are saying in the affirmation and repeat it over and over. They can be said silently or out loud. I like to, at least now and then, say them out loud as I believe this adds a little more impetus to them.

Below are a few examples of affirmations I use, but you are encouraged to compose your own to focus on the changes you want for yourself. They should be brief declarative statements that are easy to remember.

I have perfect faith (in God).

I have perfect harmony between spirit, mind, and body.
I am selfless, generous, and humble.

I have love and compassion for all people and all things.
I am loving, kind, and forgiving to all persons at all times, and in all situations and circumstances.

My personal experience has shown that this process is very effective. I encourage you to give it a try.

November 2, 2013

Faith and Spiritual Awareness

Are faith and spiritual awareness the same thing? This is an interesting question and no doubt there are many different views concerning the answer.

In thinking about this in the context of my own religious and spiritual experiences, I am of the belief that they are not the same. I see faith as a doorway or threshold through which most people must pass in order to begin a path to spiritual awareness. There are exceptions to this, but for most of us faith in a higher being is a necessary first step.

At the same time, simply believing in God is not sufficient for becoming spiritually aware. If we think about it, we realize that we know many people who participate in the rituals of organized religion but show no signs of spiritual awareness. When they walk out the door of their place of worship they leave God behind and return to their often self-centered and materialistic lifestyle. This can also apply to those who believe in God, but do not participate in organized religion.

In contrast, those with spiritual awareness see the world very differently. They see God in everything around them.

They feel his presence every minute of every day. They constantly give Him thanks and praise, and they make a very conscious effort to live a life of goodness. They hold themselves accountable for their mistakes, wrong-doing, and transgressions, and they have genuine repentance.

Living a spiritually aware life may be a paradigm shift for many people. Nevertheless, once having found the doorway to a spiritual life, do not be afraid to pass through. Keep an open mind and be prepared to make sacrifices and take on new responsibilities inherent in the knowledge you will receive.

November 10, 2013

What is Spiritual Awareness?

My personal spiritual experiences have led me to view what we mean by spiritual awareness differently than many people. Perhaps the most common and basic concept of spiritual awareness is simply an awareness of, or belief in, a higher being. I see this as a very limited and somewhat passive perspective.

My view of spiritual awareness is much more expansive and active. As discussed last week, this awareness most often begins with a belief in God, but spiritual awareness is not a belief, *it is an experience*.

As one's spiritual awareness expands beyond basic belief, things happen. One begins to have inspirations and revelations. New knowledge and/or understanding blossom within us. Sometimes knowledge we already had springs forth with a new perspective, or takes on a deeper meaning and significance. This new meaning sometimes compels us to take action of some sort.

Expanding spiritual awareness and knowledge often bring with them new responsibilities that may require personal sacrifices. An example from my own spiritual evolution was the realization and belief that it is wrong to raise animals for food. This grew out of my expanding spiritual understanding of how all life forms are interconnected with each other and with God.

I took responsibility for this revelation by committing to vegetarianism and I am now a staunch supporter of animal's rights. As one acquires more spiritual knowledge, one must adapt their thinking and behavior to reflect that knowledge. This is why I refer to spirituality as a developmental or evolutionary process.

To experience a more expansive spiritual awareness, we must truly open our minds and put aside any preconceived notions and prejudices. If we want to experience deeper levels of spiritual awareness, all we need do is ask, but we must be willing to change in response to the spiritual knowledge and understanding we receive.

November 25, 2013

Prayer: Spiritual or Self-Serving?

Prayer, for most of us, is the primary means by which we communicate with God. The question is: what should we be saying when "speaking" with Him?

It seems that many who pray use it mostly to ask for things they *want*, even though God has already provided what they *need*. This is in keeping with the self-centered, materialistic mind-set of society today.

Why should one ask for more than they need when there are so many around the world who are barely able to scratch out the most basic existence? To ask for more when we already have enough, may be offensive to God. He has a life plan for each of us and He will provide precisely what we need to support that life plan and the service to which we have been called.

I question the value of saying prayers prescribed by a religion in a long chain over and over again. The repetitive nature of this form of prayer can quickly make the process one of a mindless drone. If the first repetition was said from the heart with sincere and conscious intent, then it need not be repeated.

Saying the same prayer again and again is not likely to give it greater force. In fact, it may even have a negative effect. Who wants to hear the same thing over and over? Soon one stops listening. When you say a single prayer with all of your heart and soul, it will be heard throughout all of the heavenly spheres with clarity and power.

And praying should not be restricted to time spent at one's place of worship. Prayer should be an ongoing, frequent, daily practice said anywhere at any time. This is especially true for prayers of thanks. As a continuous process, prayer is a spiritual presence of mind where one is always aware of the presence of God in all things.

We should not make "promises" to God such that if He gives us X, then we promise to change our ways and do Y. Instead, we should attend to how we live on a daily basis, and always treat others with kindness. Then we will be rewarded without asking.

We are all human with limited ability to protect ourselves from harm and to cope with pain and suffering. If we find ourselves in a dangerous situation, or we suffer from some malady, prayer can often bring the help and strength we need to endure.

When we ask for material things for ourselves, prayer becomes a hollow self-serving exercise that may fall upon deaf ears. However, prayer becomes an expression of our spirit when we use it to give thanks for what God has chosen to give us, to ask for help for others, and to seek guidance concerning how we can be better human beings. Such prayers are *always* answered.

December 1, 2013

We Exist in the Ethereal Spaces in Between the Atoms

As noted in my first book and in previous blog entries, I believe that our true life is one of spirit. That is why I promote the idea of living a life of spirit rather than one anchored in the physical world.

We were created in spirit and will remain so forever more. Our spiritual existence does not stop or go into abeyance during the brief periods when we are clothed with a physical body. We may lose touch with our spirit-self from time to time, stupefied by the many distractions of the physical world.

But in the background, out of the din, our spirit cries out for expression. The challenge is to have the presence of mind and *desire* to hear it.

Our spirit calls to us with the sweet, soft voice of a lover, to remind us that we exist in the ethereal spaces *between* the atoms of the physical world. We are merely passersby and should consider what spiritual legacy we wish to leave behind in the physical world, because that is the only thing that will follow us when it is time move on.

While all that is composed will eventually be decomposed, our spirits will continue to exist as a part of our everlasting

Creator. Just as He has always existed and always will, so shall we in spirit form.

December 11, 2013

Eulogy on the Demise of Character

There was a time when the social, economic, and political currency was *character*. What I mean by a person of character is one who exhibits honesty, integrity, courage, and ethical behavior. How many people do you know who consistently display these attributes? Sadly, it seems they are rather scarce these days.

I knew such a person. My father who recently passed away was such a man. He was a member of the so-called "Greatest Generation." They were the people who grew up during the Great Depression and went on to fight in World War II. One of the hallmarks of the majority of that generation was steadfast honesty in business dealings as well as interpersonal interactions. I prefer to call them the Generation of *Character*.

My father was the most honest person I have ever known. He had his own business and had a reputation for honesty and integrity. He charged only what a job actually cost in terms of material and labor. He took pride in his work and used only materials of the highest quality. His profit margin was small, and his word was his bond. Moreover, he did his best to hold others to a similar standard when they provided business services or products to him.

He didn't make a lot of money, and never had or asked for a lot. Yet, he was quite content knowing that he did his best to always do the right thing in every situation. The high road came naturally to him, so there was never a dilemma concerning which path to follow. He wasn't perfect, but he got the important stuff right.

As far as I can tell, character was the mind-set of many members of the Greatest Generation—soon to be extinct. The depression and the war taught many of them humility and that God can take away all that we have at any time. It taught them to treasure family and friends, because they are with us for an indeterminate and sometimes painfully short period of time.

For my own part, I lament, not only the loss of my father, but also the loss of character in so many members of contemporary society. What descriptor will be used by historians to characterize the present generations? What legacy of lifestyle will they (we) leave for future generations? Can character ever again dominate the human psyche and way of life of the majority?

December 29, 2013

Charity Doth Call My Spirit Forth

Charity that comes from the heart is an act of love and compassion where the spirit reveals itself in all of its divine glory. It raises us up ever so slightly so that our feet seem to lose touch with the ground, if only briefly. With each charitable act, a wave of happiness and fulfillment washes over us and for those few moments, we understand the meaning and purpose of life. We realize that our joy comes from giving of ourselves—our spirit selves—to others.

But too often these moments are fleeting. When our feet touch the ground again, we find ourselves yearning to soar once more, free of the constraints, obligations, and selfish desires of the physical life. But it is not our time to fly away just yet. We must prove ourselves worthy of wings.

It is my belief that charity is a human and spiritual *responsibility*. We must strive to make charity a central part of our everyday life. Charity is an important way that we can express our spirit or spirituality. In its pure form it is an act of unselfish love and compassion with no expectation or desire for material gain or recognition.

If you make a big deal about how much you contribute to charity or about things you do to help others, you seek to raise yourself up in the eyes of others. On the other hand, if you are humble and your charity is motivated only by genuine caring for others, you raise yourself up in the eyes of God.

The charity of a spiritual person is generally done privately and seen only by those they are helping, or by the charitable foundation receiving their donations. That is to say, they do it because they see people in need and they know the right thing to do is help if they can.

January 25, 2014

Spiritual Kinship

Is there spiritual kinship among all living things, especially people? The answer to this question depends on what you believe about the nature of our existence.

As indicated in previous entries to this blog, I believe that we exist as spirit and that we all come from the same Source. In spirit form, free of the physical body, all distinctions of race, ethnicity, national origin, gender, socioeconomic status and so forth disappear.

As children of God, we are all kindred spirits with sameness likened to identical twins. In spirit form, we all "look" alike, and when first born as spirit, we all have the same potential for spiritual development.

If we genuinely understood our spiritual kinship, then we would care for all people as we care for our husbands, wives, children, and so forth. We would never allow anyone to be cold, hungry, or thirsty.

There would be no envy, struggles for advantage or power, and no greed. Rather our love for all of our spirit kin would compel us to raise others up and fulfill their needs without hesitation or thought about ourselves.

I believe that all of humanity has a spiritual kinship. The challenge is not so much to come to this realization, but rather to live in a manner that reflects such a belief.

February 1, 2014

What is Faith?

As I understand it, faith is the certainty in one's belief in some thing or someone. Of course in the context of spirituality, faith usually refers to one's certainty in the existence of a higher being, universal energy, or creator.

When we say we have faith in a person, we are letting them know that we trust them or have trust in them—trust in their abilities, trust that they will not do anything to hurt us, trust that they will be there when we need their help or support.

It could be said that our faith in God has these same attributes and expectations. However, our faith in God is intuitive and comes from spiritual awareness, whereas our faith in a person is experiential and based on concrete knowledge of their past behaviors. Consequently, faith in a higher being is a leap that some are unwilling to take.

Another form of faith refers to trust in a religious doctrine and what are believed to be God's promises and teachings found in religious scriptures. I believe that one should be cautious here and not let this type of faith to be blind. The scriptures and the clergy should not go unchallenged.

Scriptures from the various religions provide a lot of wonderful guidance concerning how to live a spiritual life of goodness. I think that most of us would independently agree on which passages provide such spiritual wisdom.

However, skepticism about other passages is healthy and may provide deeper insight. We would be remiss if we blindly accepted everything in the scriptures as the word of God. We were given the ability to reason and, if we apply it, we will be able to distinguish the word of God from those of men.

February 9, 2014

What is Salvation?

What is salvation? What does it mean to be saved? Indeed, how *is* one saved?

There are different interpretations of what salvation means. Perhaps the most popular view in the west is that Jesus, through his suffering and death, saved us from punishment by God for our sins. An extension of this in some Christian sects is that one can be saved *only* through faith in Jesus the Savior.

My concern about such beliefs is that some people, believing that they are assured of salvation by their faith, might consciously or subconsciously begin to think that how they live their life is not so important. Salvation by faith in Christ also implies exclusivity and favoritism of one group over another by God. This is not logical; God loves all of His children.

The above view of "salvation" would seem to relieve believers from accountability for their actions through intervention by someone or something *outside* of themselves. Consequently, there would be no need for one to take responsibility for wrongdoing because they would be forgiven by virtue of their religious faith.

This does not withstand the test of reason, because it suggests that it doesn't matter what one my do since salvation would avoid retribution in the afterlife. However, without consequences for wrongdoing, there would be no learning, no incentive for change, and therefore, no spiritual progression.

In fact, I question whether faith in God has anything to do with whether or not one will find the Kingdom of Heaven. Rather, I believe what is important and essential is how one lives their life and the degree to which they are able to express their spirit. It is my belief that one has to live a life of love, compassion, and virtue to experience the Kingdom of God. In other words, entry into the Kingdom of Heaven does not rely on particular religious beliefs, but rather on one's thoughts and actions.

Further, if we are to be "saved" from our transgressions, then we must save *ourselves* through right action and change. One's belief in the Kingdom of Heaven and the divinity within us should be motivators for self-improvement and actuation of the spirit. Jesus made it clear that following the spiritual laws that he taught and demonstrated about how to live and how to treat others are what will reveal the Kingdom of Heaven that exists inside each of us.

March 8, 2014

The Law of Service

The material world presents us with many challenges, not the least of which is maintaining awareness of our spiritual divinity and seeing opportunities for its expression. It's so easy to get caught up in the day-to-day of work and family.

Although these things and more can provide fertile ground for learning, many of us may not realize that God has certain expectations of us—laws to govern and guide life in the material world and when we return to the world of spirit. An extremely important one is the Law of Service. It is through actuation of this law in our lives that we express our spirit and evolve. I believe service is a requirement for progression to higher spiritual planes.

How many people do you know who engage regularly in some form of service to others? In this day and age, it seems like many of us are too engrossed in our personal lives and the quest for fame, fortune, love, or whatever else to think about helping others. As a consequence, we miss out on one of the most rewarding things in life—helping others through service.

The Law of Service is inherent in the commandment "Thou shalt love thy neighbor as thyself." Jesus said this commandment of brotherly love is second only to "Thou shalt love the Lord thy God with all thy heart, and with all thy soul, and with thy entire mind." In fact, if you believe that each of us is a part of God, then to love others is to love God and vice versa. Consequently, it could be said that the two commandments are simply different expressions of the same spiritual law.

We have a spiritual kinship with all of humanity. Therefore, people locally and around the world are our neighbors. We are expected to love them all, and in so doing, to provide service and help to anyone who needs it. Unselfish service to others is the single most important thing we can do to change the world.

March 15, 2014

The Spiritual Mind

I believe that the mind has two aspects or qualities: spiritual and intellectual. We are all familiar with the intellectual mind. It is responsible for processes like reasoning, judgment, analysis, calculation, ego, desire, and other mundane faculties. I envision the spiritual mind engaging in activities such as charity, creativity, intuition, and psychic abilities.

The two aspects of mind likely operate on different planes of consciousness. The intellectual mind (IM) focuses on the physical world, while the spiritual mind (SM) searches for meaning, and communion with God.

Worldly knowledge is acquired by the IM through study and investigation of measurable quantities. Spiritual knowledge can be obtained to some extent by study also. However, oftentimes, the most profound spiritual knowledge comes to us without active searching or any effort on our part except having an open mind and a desire to come closer to God.

Sometimes spiritual knowledge defies logic and ordinary understanding. It can come to us with an inexplicable certainty in its truth, while at the same time we do not know how we know it or from where the knowledge came to us.

The two minds look at the world and existence quite differently. The IM primarily sees the here and now, while the SM senses there is much more to existence. Dominance by the IM may lead one to deny or overlook their spiritual nature. It may also lead one to question the existence of God or a Creator, as the IM favors (perhaps requires) measurement and proof over intuition and faith.

In contrast, the SM cares little about the material aspects of existence favoring instead expression of itself through inspiration, creativity, psychic connection, and emotions such as love and compassion.

How do the two aspects of mind reconcile with one another? The IM is essential in order for us to function in the material world. The SM brings meaning to the activities of the IM. The spiritual qualities of mentality moderate and guide the IM toward applications of its faculties that will be spiritually fulfilling and serve the greater good. I believe that a key element of our spiritual progression and evolution is for the SM to achieve dominance over the IM.

I am Spirit

I am Spirit.

I have existed before time began

And I will exist after the end of time.

I am you and you are me.

I am a victim of doubt, skepticism, and ignorance.

I am present in bodies with minds that do not recognize me.

I gave life to you, but you do not truly live.

I am love—yet, you do not share me widely.

I am compassion—yet, you hide my light deep inside.

I am generous—yet, you do not give to those who are needy.

I give you knowledge, but you refuse to believe.

I show you the Path, but you turn away and choose another.

I provide good counsel, but you do not listen.

I am Spirit. I am you, and you are me.

One day you will awaken to me

And our glorious light will shine upon world!

The message here is clear: we must understand and believe that we exist as spirit, and not neglect or be afraid to express our divine qualities.

April 12, 2014

The Transformative Nature of Tragedy

Traumatic events in our lives are usually the most transformative—whether it is nearly dying, the loss of a loved one, or some other calamity. It is sad that tragedy and heartbreak are often needed to initiate positive change in many of us.

Tragedy often rekindles our compassion for others and expands our understanding of suffering. Traumatic events draw our spirit forth causing us to reach out to others, not so much to get support, as to give it. Not so much to grieve a loss, as to celebrate one life, and resolve to improve another (usually our own).

Our search for meaning in the loss of a loved one, more often than not, turns inward to seek how we can honor their memory, become better human beings, and truly live ourselves. These thoughts come, not so much from a fear of death, but rather to exalt life—to come to understand what is important in life, and in doing so, undergo a meaningful transformation for the better. The challenge is to integrate positive changes in us brought about by this transformation in a way that guides our lives continuously and irreversibly going forward.

April 20, 2014

My Companion and Me

"Are you feeling lost and downhearted," he asked? "Come, take my hand and follow me. We have been strangers for too long. Do not be afraid."

"Where are we going," I asked?

"We are going where you have always yearned to go. Come I will show you the way. The path we will walk together can be difficult, but the destination well worth it."

"This is too hard. I don't think I can do it."

"Of course you can! Focus on the light up ahead. It will give you strength. Don't you see how it gets brighter the farther we go?"

"I didn't realize how we were emerging from such a dark mist. As I look back down the path from where we came,

I see that it fades into total darkness. I did not know how lost and confused I was back there."

"We still have a long way to go, but I will be with you every step of the way. Just don't let go of my hand or lose sight of the expanding light ahead."

"As we continue to progress, I feel closer and closer to you."

"I have always been a part of you waiting for you to take notice. Now that you have acknowledged me, we can continue the journey truly as one, fearless with great strength and conviction."

****

Jesus taught us that the Kingdom of God is within each of us, and it is realized through love, compassion, and forgiveness. Get in touch with your own divinity and show it to the world!

June 14, 2014

Can Love Save the World?

It seems everyone is obsessed with looking for love these days, whether it is a physical hookup or the search for a soul mate. Either way the focus is on one's self. Most of us have this backwards. We should be *giving* love to those all around us. This will, in turn, attract love to us.

Restricting our love to spouse, family, and friends is not sufficient for spiritual progression and does not fulfill our divine capacity and responsibility to love broadly. Radiating our divine love to all we encounter is the ultimate expression of our spirit and spirituality.

We have all heard the cliché "Only love can save the world." This is one of those truths that sadly will remain a cliché until we begin to take it seriously and apply it globally in our everyday lives. If you want to change the world your love has to flow out *away* from yourself to everyone around you including total strangers.

I acknowledge that this is not always easy, especially when someone is being unmanageable. But we need to try to not react, and simply radiate love and kindness. Sometimes this will disarm the one acting up; sometimes it will not. Nevertheless, we need to make the effort, because the intent behind actions is what they will be measured against in the spiritual realms. If your genuine intent was to give love freely and it was rejected, you still benefit spiritually from your efforts. You will acquire spiritual capital that will help you going forward.

You may wonder, how loving globally can change the world. It can do so over time by *setting an example* that inspires others to follow. When they see the effect your loving ways have on them and others, they will want to give the same happiness to people they encounter and feel the joy and fulfillment that they see in you.

Feeling love and compassion for others, although noble, serves no one if it is not expressed through *action*. When we become aware of people or animals who need help in our neighborhood, on TV, or otherwise, then we need to *do* something. Make a phone call, knock on a door, lend a helping hand, say a prayer, or donate money or time.

As we move through our day, we need to make an effort to see beyond ourselves, and our own selfish needs and desires. We need to be nice to people and show kindness to others, even if they are being a bit difficult.

All of us should take the time to give serious thought to what the world would be like if the majority focused on helping others, rather than pursuing their own fame, fortune, and love life. After thinking about this, you may conclude that love can indeed save the world.

July 14, 2014

The Reluctant Goodbye

There he lay on his death bed. He had a wonderful life of failure and triumph, sorrow and joy, as well as disappointment and blessings. As he reflected on his life, he began to have feelings of profound loss. Not because of regret or for the things that might have been, but because of having to leave behind those he loves.

He had said his difficult goodbyes to other members of the family. Only the youngest two members remained to be seen for the last time.

Saving them for last seemed apt: as one road comes to an end, another begins. It provided a reminder of just how far he had come from the innocence of childhood to the spiritual trials of adulthood, and finally to the enlightened end of a long life well lived.

As these thoughts washed through his mind, his two youngest grandchildren came into the room to visit. They were quite young—barely in grade school. They were too young to have a grasp of what it means to die. He struggled with how to tell them he was going to have to leave them.

"Come here you two. Get in the bed with me," he said. "I was hoping you would come to see me today."

The two of them, a boy and a girl, climbed up into the bed—one on each side—and laid their heads on his chest. As they did this, a powerful wave of love welled up inside him and he had to force back the tears that strained to explode forth under the force of his emotions. He did not want to ruin these last moments with these two that he loved so much.

For a few minutes he could not speak. Then he said, "There is something I want the two of you to know. I love you both more than anything, but I must go away and I will not see you again for a long time. I don't want to leave you, but sometimes we must do things that we would rather not do. I want you to know that when I am gone I continue to love you, just like you love me when we are apart, right?"

In unison they said, "Yes grandpa."

"Always remember the fun we had and how much I love you. While we are apart, you will be wrapped in a blanket of my love that will keep you warm and safe always. Does that sound good?"

"Yes grandpa," they replied.

"But when will we see you again?" asked the little girl.

"I don't know when you will see me, but I will always be with you because of the love that we have for each other."

The little boy said, "I love you grandpa. I'm going to miss you."

"Me too," said the little girl.

"I can't begin to tell you how much I am going to miss you guys. I will be watching over you from afar and I will

58

always be with you in your hearts and minds, and you will always be in mine."

When the children left and the door closed behind them, he closed his eyes and drifted away. He left behind tears running down his check for the sorrow his departure will cause, and a smile of gratitude on his face for finally getting it right.

July 27, 2014

The Privilege of Special Abilities

The human race has not accessed or expressed its full potential regarding powers of the mind and body. No wonder considering that so few of us appear to have expressed the third aspect of being—the spirit-self.

I believe that humanity has indeed tapped into only a tiny fraction of its physical and mental abilities. Any uncommon, extraordinary, or special abilities or powers that we observe in a small percentage of the population provide a glimpse into some of the amazing human potential that lays dormant in all of us.

I must stress *potential* because, as noted, only a very few have extraordinary abilities, and usually only one special ability exists in an individual. Perhaps someday, special abilities will become more commonplace. However, it may require many millennia of spiritual evolution of the human species before this can happen.

Why is it that we cannot access and express the full range of special abilities that we know to exist, as well as a host of others of which we are not yet aware? I believe that the human race is not spiritually ready for the awesome power that lies latent within it. Humanity's potential power will gradually unfold and express in accord with its level of spiritual progression and evolution. We must as a species demonstrate that we understand the responsibility that comes with knowledge and special abilities. That is, we are expected to use these only for good and to unselfishly help, heal, inspire, and uplift our fellow human beings.

We can begin to see the danger in jumping ahead too quickly. Man had progressed in his scientific knowledge and ability to learn how to split the atom. However, he was not ready spiritually to use its power only for good. Instead, one of the first applications of that knowledge was to make an atomic bomb.

Although extraordinary and special abilities are seen to manifest physically, I believe that they are actually powers of the spirit that are being expressed through the body. The privilege of such power must be earned. In order for uncommon abilities to be expressed, one must be at a level of spiritual awareness and evolution that is sufficient to assure that they will be used responsibly.

September 26, 2014

On the Nature of God

Who or what is God? The qualities that we imagine God or a higher being would have are to some extent a paradox, enigmatic, and most certainly beyond our limited awareness and understanding. I wondered about the nature of God, and when I sat down to write the following came out.

The All Powerful Unknowable

I am the uncreated One.

I exist apart from the bounds of time.

I am beyond beginning and end

For I have always existed and always will.

I am both the Creator, and the created.

I made everything in the universe.

I am everywhere and in all things.

I cannot be created or destroyed.

I can transform myself into countless forms.

Yet, I am without form.

I am unknowable and unseen, but everywhere you look.

I am Love which is testimony to my existence!

November 6, 2014

With Spirit Eyes I See...

With spirit eyes I see *you*...

With spirit eyes I see you and I are kindred spirits.

With spirit eyes I see we are all connected parts of a whole.

With spirit eyes I see many paths leading to higher levels of spiritual awareness.

With spirit eyes I see a powerful being unaware of its spirit-self.

With spirit eyes I see your spirit body (the real you)—so beautiful and perfect.

With spirit eyes I see your potential for unconditional love for all living things.

With spirit eyes I see *me*...

With spirit eyes I clearly see and understand my transgressions.

With spirit eyes I see that my suffering can lead to redemption and greater awareness.

With spirit eyes I see the invisible ones always close at hand to help me.

With spirit eyes I see the beautiful light and love that radiates from them.

With spirit eyes I see that my purpose is to serve.

With spirit eyes I see that this is what gives life meaning.

November 30, 2014

The Spiritual Experience of Knowing

What is the spiritual experience of Knowing and how does it differ from religious faith or belief? I will try to answer these questions based on my own spiritual experiences. It is an event that may be difficult to grasp through description, and for some difficult to believe without experiencing it themselves.

The spiritual type of knowing discussed here does not refer to factual knowledge, languages, or memory. Rather, as used here, it refers to an inexplicable revelation of spiritual truths of which one suddenly somehow *knows* with *absolute certainty.*

The Knowing may take place in a brief, spontaneous altered state of consciousness, or simply by an abrupt, strong flood of thought. Either is sure to get one's attention and there will be no doubt that something extraordinary has occurred. The knowledge given in this manner may be previously unknown to the recipient, or it may involve something of which the recipient had prior knowledge, but which had not yet taken deep root in their awareness.

A characteristic aspect of this type of knowing is that it is unexpected, and sometimes powerful and overwhelming. *It is a spiritual* **experience** unlike anything you may have witnessed before. This is in contrast to faith and belief which are somewhat abstract, intentional commitments that one makes regarding religious and spiritual matters. That is not to say that spiritual experience cannot arise from foundations of faith, but rather faith and belief are not experiences in and of themselves.

For example, one may have faith and believe that there is a God, accepting His existence as a concept. Whereas, a Knowing would be to palpably *experience* His presence and qualities in an altered state of awareness.

In my first book, I describe some of my spiritual experiences of Knowing. Each one was transformative and together they have changed the way I live, think, and view the world. They provided much of the impetus for the writing found on this website.

The experience of Knowing is not something that one can willfully create. One must be spiritually ready to receive the knowledge it brings. A Knowing is a spontaneous event for which the factors or circumstances needed for its occurrence are unknown. It is my belief that if one has an open mind concerning spirituality, a genuine desire for spiritual truth, and strives for purity of heart that they may become fertile ground for the spiritual experience of Knowing.

December 27, 2014

The Quintessence of Life

What is the quintessence of life—that magical elixir from which all life arose and which fills it with jubilation? What is the highest, most noble element that is pervasive throughout the heavenly realms?

I believe that *love* is the fundamental component of all planes of existence. Love is an uncreated *spiritual quality* that is a healing, nurturing, fulfilling, and guiding force. It is the primordial element from which we arose and to which we shall return.

Divine love comes from without (from God and the holy spirits that serve him) and it comes from within (from the divinity of our spirit-selves). It is all encompassing and encompassed by all.

Love is the greatest of all commandments. The purpose of our journeys through the millennia is, in large part, to come to understand that we are capable of unconditional love for all things, and once realized, to radiate that love through expression of our spirit-selves.

After many lifetimes our spirit will emerge to full expression and our love for all things truly will have no bounds or conditions. When that happens, our earth journey may well end returning our spirit to its most basic existence—one that simply radiates divine love forever.

Love transcends matter, space, and time. It is foremost among the spiritual mysteries, and a treasured gift from God that is meant to be shared with all.

January 13, 2015

The Accidental Ascetic

Over the last several years I have become an ascetic of sorts. It was not a conscious decision or goal; rather, it was a natural progression of an evolving spirituality and lifestyle.

I acknowledge that what I am about to describe is not for everyone and I am not suggesting that anyone should try to emulate my path. Each of us will be led down our respective spiritual paths naturally.

My children have on occasion half-jokingly (or half seriously) pictured me as a Buddhist monk or similar, cloistered in my home practicing qigong and tai chi and burning incense. The fact is I do keep largely to myself and practice the above Asian energy arts daily. I also pray on and off as I move through my day as things come to mind. But these things are only a part of my life, not its totality.

Becoming a vegetarian was a key step in my accidental progression toward asceticism. Denying myself of the many foods that I once enjoyed, especially animal flesh, was cleansing, not only for my body, but also for my spirit. I surprised myself with the determination and total commitment and conviction that I brought to the challenge. It showed me an inner strength of which I was not aware.

However, my vegetarianism did not arise for the sake of self-sacrifice or asceticism. Instead, it came from a strong belief that it is wrong to raise animals in large numbers for food. I could no longer support the barbaric treatment of farmed animals.

I have been vegetarian for almost three years now and I have never wavered from my pledge. One of the collateral outcomes of my vegetarianism was a very limited menu of only a few dishes that I prepare for myself—nevertheless, much better than the tasteless porridge some monks may have to eat.

Another incidental outcome is that I rarely eat in restaurants because gluten-free vegetarian meals are rare or non-existent at most eating establishments. This also makes it difficult to travel which is something I've had to curtail.

But my so-called asceticism goes further. For example, I care little about material things. I have no desire to further enrich myself with money, things, recognition, or position. Furthermore, I am not the least bit impressed by those who seek notice for what they have or appear to have. However, I *do* take notice of those in need and support a number of charities throughout the year.

Part of (or perhaps as a result of) my apparent asceticism is a gradual shift away from things of the material world to the things of spirit. That is, a shift to spiritual values and seeing the world through spirit eyes. For me, this is the value and benefit of moving toward a somewhat ascetic way of life.

Although far from the true ascetic, the degree of asceticism that characterizes my life now helps me to put things in proper perspective and to see myself *within and among* the sea of humanity, not detached, beyond, or above it. I see our collective and individual suffering and wish to somehow ease it through healing, service, and prayer.

The purpose of life, both in body and spirit form, is to serve others with love and compassion. Doing so is what gives our lives meaning, and what demonstrates the divinity within each and every one of us.

March 6, 2015

From What Purpose Comes Meaning?

"Teacher, why am I here?" I asked.

"You are here to change the world," the teacher replied in a matter-of-fact tone.

Taken aback I asked, "How can I change the world when I am only *one* among *billions*?"

"Ah, but you are not alone in this," he said. "There are many like you around the world seeking to expand their spiritual awareness. There are even more who seek meaning for their lives, but are not yet spiritually aware."

"But teacher, what is it that gives life meaning, or perhaps I should say: what is the meaning of life?" I wondered.

He smiled as a parent might to a child's simple-minded question and replied, "There are some who seek meaning by pursuing a career. Others seek meaning through their family life. Still others seek meaning through devotion to their religion, but the answer is much more basic than these things."

"I can see where one could get some measure of satisfaction and fulfillment from each of these," I said.

"Yes, but there is something more fundamental that brings meaning to these and all human endeavors," replied the teacher.

Not understanding where the teacher was going with this, I asked, "What is more basic than making one's way in the world, love of family, and devotion to God?" When I heard his answer, I felt as if I were indeed a naive child again.

He said, "You must understand that all of the children of Earth have kinship with one another. All of humanity arose from one and the same God the Father. Consequently, you are expected to give all persons you meet the same love and compassion that you would to your own parents, siblings, children, etc. It is helping and serving others that is most fulfilling and that gives life its true meaning."

Trying to grasp a deeper understanding of what the teacher was saying, I declared, "So what you are saying is that love and compassion should underlie and guide all human interactions."

"Yes, that is why you are here! That is how you will change the world! That is your life's purpose!" he said. "This is the lesson that humanity must learn!"

April 5, 2015

Prayers for Harmony

Prayer for World Harmony

Heavenly Father,

I pray for peace, harmony, security, equality, and freedom for all of the children of Earth.

They long for the time when goodness and light will once again prevail over the evil and darkness which have ruled the Earth for far too long.

I pray that your sacred light will continually grow ever brighter and purge the Earth of all shadows and darkness where evil abides.

May your children come to understand that their salvation will not come through blind adherence to the doctrines and edicts of their religious faith.

But rather, simply by loving you and living a life of unselfish goodness and virtue.

May harmony between spirit, mind, and body found by one extend to the many and result in peace among nations and a spiritual renewal and awakening of the people of the world. Lord hear my prayer!

The foregoing expresses aspirations for all people. The following prayer seeks harmony within us as individuals.

71

Prayer for Harmony

Dear God,

I strive to make myself whole, and by doing so come closer to you.

I wish to find the sacred harmony between spirit, mind, and body.

My only desire is to serve and honor you by expression of my spirit through acts of love and compassion.

I pray that my spirit may one day become attuned with, and radiate your divine love for all things. Amen

May 25, 2015

Spiritual Lawlessness

The state of much of the world today can be characterized as spiritual lawlessness. What this means in large part is that basic laws of human behavior such as honesty, integrity, morality, and ethics are being ignored—or worse—not being taught or modeled to our children. This type of lawlessness is a sure sign of a declining civilization. It is indicative of a society that allowed it to become lost in a spiritual wasteland.

Spiritual lawlessness is a failure to apply the basic principles that underlie living a life of goodness. It also represents a failure to be mindful of the Ten Commandments and spiritual laws such as the laws of cause and effect, and retribution and compensation. It seems that a great many people have lost touch with these time-honored guiding principles.

These natural laws have guided human behavior and inter-actions for millennia. Are generations now living going to be the ones who allow the most basic of God's laws to be ignored and perhaps eventually lost in history?

There are many comparatively trivial societal laws with which almost everyone complies. For example, we all know that a red light means stop. We stop automatically because, if we do not, we believe that we will either get a costly ticket or cause an accident that could be fatal.

Yet, it appears that many who were taught the Ten Commandments as a child have since "forgotten" them even though violating them will bring grievous harm to them spiritually. Some may willfully disregard them because compliance would deprive them of serving their own selfish desires. While others may have lost sight of them due to societal pressure to conform to widespread materialism and pursuit of self-interests.

Many of us have fallen prey to sophisticated marketing campaigns and programming that loosened restrictions on the depiction of violence and sexual depravity. As a result, the psyche of people in developed countries around the

73

world was taken down a dark path of spiritual depravation and lawlessness.

It is my hope that those who are not happy about the state of society will take a few minutes to not only read the Ten Commandments, but reflect upon their application in the context of today's society and the many situations in which we see violations. It is easy to quickly glance over them and assume that you "know" them. However, a more thoughtful and deeper reading would be most beneficial.

I have given a few examples below to help us begin thinking about their practical applications. As an example, let us look at the commandment *"Thou shalt not steal."* This is not just about things like shop lifting or burglary. We see many kinds of theft in today's society. For example, over charging for goods and services by setting very high profit margins, putting forth another person's work as your own, theft of proprietary systems, processes, and recipes to name a few.

Another commandment is *"Thou shalt not bear false witness against thy neighbor."* It is tempting to shirt past this one because superficially it sounds like something that applies to a courtroom. In the broadest terms, what it says to me is to not spread lies about others. We shouldn't lie about what we may have seen or heard. We shouldn't try to shift blame to someone else for something we did.

Thou shalt not covet things that others have is the gist of Commandment 10. I do not see any redeeming quality in being jealous of or longing for what others have. Doing so will likely lead you to unhappiness and dissatisfaction. I believe we should be grateful for what we have and stay within our financial means.

I encourage everyone to do their own analysis of practical situations where each commandment applies to human behavior today. It is an exercise that may be valuable for bringing the Ten Commandments back to the forefront of our minds and signal a red light when we get into situations where they apply. This will give us a chance to carefully consider how to proceed.

Spiritual lawlessness has cast a dark shadow over the world. Let us each do our part to make sure that we do not participate in it by always being mindful of God's commandments and natural laws. He gives us so much while asking precious little in precious in return.

June 2, 2015

A Presence Palpable

I believe that God should be a part of our every waking moment—a presence palpable. We should honor Him and pay homage to him throughout our day. We can do this in many ways. A very important one is for goodness to permeate our every thought and action. Working and living for good encompasses selflessness, a strong desire to help others whenever we can, and when needed, self-sacrifice to serve others before ourselves.

The attribute of goodness is a state of elevated spiritual being and connection with God. It is an expression of our spirit-selves. Inherent in (and requisite for) a life of goodness is compliance with Gods commandments and mindfulness of His natural laws.

We also honor God by being present in the moments of our day so that we take notice of the beauty and wonders of nature all around us even in the most mundane setting. When we do this, we begin to see the beauty of God Himself, in that He *is*, and is *in* all things. On these occa-sions, our spirits soar toward the heavens, even if only for those few precious moments. We cannot help but yearn for more of such time on the wind.

In addition to these ways of daily living, we should also set aside time (preferably a day) each week for rest and relaxation to recuperate from the demands of family and work. In other words, we should always remember the Sabbath and use the time to seek greater spiritual under-standing and insight. I believe this time is meant to be spent in a quiet place alone with our thoughts rather than at a place of worship with its many distractions.

This is a time where we devote ourselves to reflection and contemplation about spiritual matters and how it is that we are living our lives. It is a time for obeisance and communion with God. It should be a time when He is a presence palpable, rather than abstract idea.

June 6, 2015

One Man's Sabbath

This man's Sabbath begins looking out my kitchen windows at the beautiful golden early morning light shining through the trees. I think about how beautiful it is and wonder how much more beautiful it would be in heaven.

I watch the swirls, ripples, and reflection of light in the lovely blue water and imagine that the quality of spirit may be likened to that of water— free flowing and yielding; yet, its flow cannot be stopped by anything in its path as any impediments will eventually yield to its power.

I get in touch with my body and its internal energy as I do my daily tai chi and qigong practice. At the same time, I listen to the birds' songs heralding the new day.

Before breakfast I say my morning prayers which include prayers for healing for all who suffer around the world, and for spiritual awakening and transformation for those who have lost their way in the darkness. Lastly, I pray for mercy for all those who have, are, or will be directly affected by the many disasters and tragedies that have been happening around the world. I also ask for healing for the survivors, for those who lost loved ones, and for those who must start their lives over.

I usually listen to popular music in the background during the day when I am home. However, on this day, I listen to soft instrumental music that does not demand my attention and ideally gives a somewhat ethereal ambiance.

I try to free my mind from worldly concerns or desires and focus on spiritual matters. I usually have no plans for the day and just embrace the quiet and solitude. I may read from a diversity of religious books and writings to mine for spiritual truths and expand my spiritual vision.

The evening meal marks the end of this man's Sabbath along with a conscious desire and intent to continue this day's devotions throughout the coming week.

July 12, 2015

One Religion or No Religion?

Below is a contemporary view of the *Essentials of Judaism*, at least as seen by the religious body indicated. I found it interesting to note much overlap with some Christian and other religious beliefs as well as those of some persons (myself included) with no religious affiliations who describe themselves as spiritual. It is an excerpt from a public domain book titled *Judaism* by Israel Abrahams. The book seeks to track changes and their origins in Judaism since the early centuries of Christianity.

> A tract, entitled 'Essentials of Judaism,' has been issued in London by the Jewish Religious Union. The author, N. S. Joseph, is careful to explain that he is not putting forth these principles as 'dogmatic Articles of Faith,' and that they are solely 'suggestive outlines of belief which may be gradually imparted to children, the outlines being afterwards filled up by the teacher. But the eight paragraphs of these Essentials are at once so ably compiled and so informing as to the modern trend of Jewish belief that they will be here cited without comment.
>
> According then to this presentation, the Essentials of Judaism are:
>
> (i) There is One Eternal God, who is the sole Origin of all things and forces, and the Source of all living souls. He rules the universe with justice, righteousness, mercy, and love.
>
> (ii) Our souls, emanating from God, are immortal, and will return to Him when our life on earth ceases. While we are here, our souls can hold direct communion with God in prayer and praise, and in silent contemplation and admiration of His works.

(iii) Our souls are directly responsible to God for the work of our life on earth. God, being All-merciful, will judge us with loving-kindness, and being All-just, will allow for our imperfections; and we, therefore, need no mediator and no vicarious atonement to ensure the future welfare of our souls.

(iv) God is the one and only God. He is eternal and omnipresent. He not only pervades the entire world, but is also within us; and His Spirit helps and leads us towards goodness and truth.

(v) Duty should be the moving force of our life; and the thought that God is always in us and about us should incite us to lead good and beneficent lives, showing our love of God by loving our fellow-creatures, and working for their happiness and betterment with all our might.

(vi) In various bygone times God has revealed, and even in our own days continues to reveal to us, something of His nature and will, by inspiring the best and wisest minds with noble thoughts and new ideas, to be conveyed to us in words, so that this world may constantly improve and grow happier and better.

(vii) Long ago some of our forefathers were thus inspired, and they handed down to us—and through us to the world at large—some of God's choicest gifts,

the principles of Religion and Morality, now record-
ed in our Bible; and these spiritual gifts of God have
gradually spread among our fellow-men, so that
much of our religion and of its morality has been
adopted by them.

(viii) Till the main religious and moral principles of
Judaism have been accepted by the world at large,
the maintenance by the Jews of a separate corporate
existence is a religious duty incumbent upon them.
They are the "witnesses" of God, and they must
adhere to their religion, showing forth its truth and
excellence to all mankind. This has been and is and
will continue to be their mission. Their public worship and private virtues must be the outward man-
ifestation of the fulfillment of that mission.'

Comment

Reading this buoys my belief that a gradual convergence of
spiritual thought among the people of the world is occur-
ring. Humanity's spiritual growth, progression, and awareness going forward through the ages may well result, not so
much in a single religion, as in a single set of spiritual beliefs that have outgrown the need for the doctrines and
rituals associated with organized religion. While this may
give the clergy reason for pause, I believe it is good news
for humanity because it hearkens toward a common moral
code and understanding of the nature and purpose of our
existence.

July 21, 2015

I Can Imagine...

I can imagine that God is like water...

I am certain that I see Him moving in the flow and swirls.

I feel Him all around me gently embracing me.

I am weightless in His arms as He buoys me up so that I keep sight of the destination ahead.

He carries me when I am tired.

He is forgiving as I move through His ethereal essence.

Turbulent when His natural flow is resisted.

He slows my forward movement

To assure my progress is deliberate and considered.

I am certain that I hear Him gently calling me

To surrender to the natural flow that will take me home to Him at last!

August 16, 2015

Let Us Give Thanks

I believe that we should always express thanks and gratitude to God for all that we have, whether considered meager, grand, or something in between. Sometimes what may seem meager can be a greater blessing than that which seems grand.

In addition to giving thanks, I think it is important to demonstrate how much we value and appreciate the gifts we receive by taking adequate care of them and not take them for granted. Material things should be scrupulously maintained. Nonmaterial gifts should be nurtured, developed, and used only for good.

If we have a house or a car and we let them get run down due to neglect, then clearly we send a message of arrogance and presumption. If we take our friends and family for granted, then we dishonor them, ourselves, and God. If we are aware that we have special talents and do not use and develop them, or become arrogant and self aggrandized, then we show disdain rather than gratitude.

We like to take credit for our accomplishments and success. Of course, these require determination and hard work, but it is God who makes our success possible. After all, it is He who imbues us with our special talents, and who opens the doors of opportunity. We should always acknowledge his blessings and gifts with humility.

Let us not forget one of our greatest gifts—our body. A healthy body is one of the essential components for achieving harmony between spirit, mind, and body. It too should never be taken for granted. Neglect of the body is a sign of a disheveled spirit, a lack of respect for one's self, and ingratitude to God for the life He gave us.

I believe we have an obligation to maintain and care for our bodies. We need to keep our bodies clean, well groomed, and fit, not for the sake of vanity, but to demonstrate our gratitude to God for the body He gave us. We should do everything we can to keep our bodies healthy and free of disease, including following a healthy diet, and not overeating.

Finally, we need to show love, respect, and appreciation for the earth and all of its inhabitants. The metaphor of the earth as our mother is very appropriate since she provides sanctuary and nurture for all living things. She provides everything we need and shelters us from the unforgiving vacuum and death rays of space.

But we need to care for her just as she does us and not take her bounty and protection for granted. Just like our human mothers, she needs our love, help, and support. Her bounty has limits that we must understand and respect. She is not here to only serve humanity, but rather to promote harmony among all living things through their mutual interdependence upon one another.

We have an obligation to conserve her resources, and protect all of her "offspring." She is perhaps the most wondrous of all gifts from God since it is she who sustains us in this life.

Our gratitude for the things that God gives us, both large and small, should be ongoing through daily expression of thanks and humility, and by treasuring all the gifts and blessings we receive. That is, we should be in a constant state of grateful awe. When we are truly grateful to God and make it a point to let Him know, then we give Him the reverence He so greatly deserves.

October 26, 2015

On the Pursuit of Happiness

The pursuit of happiness leads far too many people down countless blind alleys and confusing twists and turns. Just when we think we have found the key, it vanishes leaving us once again feeling empty and unfulfilled.

Placing a high value on material things and living a material lifestyle naturally leads one to seek happiness from material things. A common misconception is that if I had a new car, or could buy a house, or had more money, or could find the love of my life, or get my dream job, etc. then I would finally be happy.

But each of us has proven this approach and vision of happiness to be false. For many of us, it is easier to identify worldly things and circumstances that might make us happy, rather than doing the soul-searching needed to understand how personal happiness can be nurtured.

None of these worldly things bring genuine, lasting happiness. One reason for this is that such things are transitory, and subject to changes in circumstances that are out of our control. Each of us is responsible for our own happiness. It cannot be given to us by something or someone else.

That said, then how does one find true happiness? What exactly does it mean to be truly happy? I believe that true happiness can only be found within ourselves and exists independent of the world around us. Happiness is a reflection of the state of our spirit-selves. Those who have achieved harmony between spirit, mind, and body have found the key to happiness.

I believe that happiness is a natural result of spiritual fulfillment. Nothing brings a greater sense of fulfillment, satisfaction, and purpose than expression of our spirit through love and compassion, and helping others. Reflecting on this, we all know it is true. Loving and helping others brings jubilation like nothing else can. Therefore, we all know that this is the key to deep and meaningful happiness.

The challenge we all face is keeping the spiritual perspective of happiness always foremost in our minds. We must constantly strive to reorder our lives, values, and priorities to pursue spiritual fulfillment and progression, rather than worldly pleasures, satisfaction, and status.

Deep inside we all know the right path for the pursuit of happiness. How many of us can muster the conviction and determination we need to take and stay on that path?

November 8, 2015

The Golden Morning

I love the golden morning light.

It's warm glow so beautiful.

And when it touches me

It feels so soft and satisfying,

Like a lover's caress.

I imagine that the hand of God is touching me and I am amidst His presence, feeling His loving embrace.

As the golden morning turns to the brightness of a sun rising higher,

My spirit rejoices and I am filled with joy!

The gentle warmth of the early hours has set the tenor of my day!

December 9, 2015

The Qur'an through the Eyes of a Non-Muslim

As part of my study of other religions and what each has to offer concerning an expanded spirituality, I recently finished reading *The Qur'an*. There are many books about *The Qur'an* and some seek to distill it down or interpret it for the reader. I wanted to read the full text myself and form my own impressions about its meaning and signif-icance. The following discussion reflects my personal understanding of the main thrust of *The Qur'an* through the eyes of a non-Muslim.

I think reading the original and forming one's own opinions about it is especially important in today's environment of fear, distrust, and even hatred for Muslims stemming from the horrific actions of so-called Islamic extremists. This is in many ways a misnomer because the actions of extremists are neither called for nor condoned by *The Qur'an*. Therefore, their self-described devotion to Islam is belied by their actions.

So what are the main teachings of *The Qur'an* as seen through the eyes of this non-Muslim? First, it is made clear that *The Qur'an* was sent to reaffirm the earlier teachings of *The Torah* and *The New Testament* concerning how to live a spiritual life. *The Qur'an* places Muslims among the descendants of Abraham and frequently cites stories from the Old Testament about Abraham, Noah, and others to illustrate points of teaching.

I found *The Qur'an* to be very repetitive with regard to its main messages. In my view, the primary message is that there is only one God who made heaven and earth, is all-knowing, all powerful, merciful, and has dominion over all things. Other recurring precepts are that there will be a resurrection of souls, and a final Day of Judgement. Those who lived a life of goodness will receive rewards in the hereafter, and those who refused to believe the above will find nothing but torment in the fires of hell. The foregoing doctrines are found in virtually every surah of *The Qur'an*.

The Qur'an describes itself as good news for those who believe and a strong warning for the disbelievers. It makes it clear that it is not our place to punish the disbelievers; that is God's right alone. Further, the reference to dis-believers does not refer to non-Muslims; it refers to all who do not believe in the one true God, resurrection, and the Day of Judgement. *The Qur'an* originated at a time in history when much of the Arabic population followed polytheist beliefs.

From the point of view of a Muslim, what I have derived from *The Qur'an* may be seen as an over simplification. I hope nothing I have said will be in any way offensive to anyone. It is just one man's condensed view of a religion rich in tradition and devotion.

Muslims, Christians, and Jews share common roots and in fact have a spiritual kinship. I think the main teachings of Islam shared by these religions of Abrahamic origin, will always remain salient, timeless, and universal. I do not believe that there is only one true/correct religion; rather, I believe there is only one true God who wishes to guide us all to the path of goodness, virtue, and everlasting life.

Reference

Haleem, M.A.S. Abdel., *trans., The Qur'an.* Oxford: Oxford University Press, 2010. First published 2004.

February 7, 2016

Buddhism: Spirituality for Everyone Part 1

I have been curious about Buddhism ever since years ago reading *Siddhartha,* the story of the life of Buddha. As a spiritual practice, Buddhism seemed somewhat mysterious, esoteric, and complex. All this talk about oneness, and remaining unattached perplexed and confused me. At the same time, there was something about it that was very intriguing.

Now having done some reading about the teachings of Buddhism I would like to share with you what I took away as some of its central teachings that have informed my quest for a deeper and expanded understanding of how to live a spiritual life.

In my view, Buddhism is in many ways a spiritual practice in its purest, most highly developed form. I say this in part because it is not a religion. Buddha is not a deity.

Buddhism is a spiritual way of living, and of conceiving the world and existence. It does not exclude or renounce a higher being; rather, practice of the concepts of Buddhism can serve as an adjunct or complement to any religion or for the nonreligious. For example, Buddhist belief and practice emphasizes universal love and compassion for all living things.

Buddhism is a very deep and challenging practice with many elements and layers that takes many years of study to comprehend and master. What I share in this and the next article to follow are but two areas of Buddhist teaching that I found interesting and especially informative to living a spiritual life.

The Four Immeasurable Minds

The Four Immeasurable Minds also are called the Four Divine States of Mind or the Four Perfect Virtues. They are said to be purifying states of mind that can transform the world. This is an area of Buddhist teaching that immediately captured my interest because these four virtues embody what I believe to be key attributes of spirituality.

The Immeasurables are:

1. Love

2. Compassion

3. Empathetic Joy

4. Equanimity

These four states of mind and being are said to be at the core of an enlightened person. They guide and empower everything that an enlightened one does and their interplay and application create conditions for progression to the highest levels of spirituality. To practice these effectively one must go beyond self and extinguish the ego.

These divine virtues are meant to be applied not only locally in everyday life, but also to be radiated in all directions throughout the world in meditation and/or prayer. In doing so, one is in communion with God.

Love or Loving-Kindness

One must live in a way that radiates immeasurable love throughout the world to all living things, unconditionally without attachment or preference for one over another.

Compassion

Similarly, one's compassion for all living things should be boundless and pervasive without discrimination or favor for one over another. It is a sincere desire that the suffering of all living things will diminish or end.

Joy or Empathetic Joy

This is selfless, measureless joy in the happiness and good fortune of all living things.

Equanimity

Equanimity is a clear, tranquil, unselfish state of mind that is free from discrimination and prejudice and holds no enmity for any living thing. It is this state of mind that fosters, facilitates, and supports love, compassion, and sym-pathetic joy that are all pervasive. In a world filled with selfishness, greed, self-aggrandizement, and racial, ethnic, and religious discrimination, the Four Immeasurables represent a major paradigm shift. Nevertheless, instilling in one's self the Four Immeasurable Minds should be the goal of anyone who wishes to be an authentic spiritual person. What a wonderful world it would be if everyone (or at least a majority) patterned their thinking and actions according to these four states of mind!

References

Brahmavihara. Wikipedia.org. Accessed February 6, 2016.

Hanh, Thic Nhat, *The Heart of the Buddha's Teaching. Transforming Suffering into Peace, Joy, and Liberation.* New York: Harmony Books. 2010. First published 1999.

The Four Immeasurables: Love, Compassion, Joy, and Equanimity. Viewonbuddhism.org. Accessed February 6, 2016.

Rahula, Walpola, *What the Buddha Taught. 2nd ed. enlarge.* New York: Grove Press. 1974. First published 1959.

February 12, 2016

Buddhism: Spirituality for Everyone Part 2

In my first article on Buddhism, we examined the Four Immeasurable Minds. These may be best described as highly elevated spiritual states of mind or ways of being. The Noble Eightfold Path discussed here can be thought of as a practical guide for living a noble and virtuous life.

The two are interrelated and interactive. Progress toward one fosters progress in the other. When both are present in an individual, the person is not only truly enlightened, but they serve as a role model for those wishing to achieve the highest levels of spirituality.

Some may worry that the Four Immeasurables may be too much of a paradigm shift to achieve or consistently sustain in a world culture that seems to be diametrically opposed to them. Such a shift in one's state of mind is indeed challenging, but it is a goal well worth pursuing.

The Noble Eightfold Path gives us practical goals for how we should strive to live our everyday lives in a manner that leads to spiritual awakening and liberation from a mind-set of greed, hatred, violence, duplicity, and self-aggrandizement. It is a path that can transform us spiritually and prepare us for progression to the divine state of the Four Immeasurable Minds.

The Noble Eightfold Path

The word "right" in this context means "in the right and most beneficial or positive way."

1. Right View or Understanding.

Right view is seeing and understanding things clearly as they truly are. It is also the ability to distinguish between thoughts and actions that are wholesome or unwholesome. Right view requires a flexible, open mind. It leads to an understanding of the law of cause and effect or moral law of karma; namely, that any action will produce results or affects that have the same nature as the original action.

2. Right Thinking, Thought, or Intention.

We need to free our minds from bias, prejudice, wrong perceptions, making assumptions, and judging. Through right thought one makes an effort to rid one's self from what they know to be wrong or immoral. In so doing, we are making a commitment to follow a spiritual path. Right thinking leads to right speech and right action.

3. Right Speech.

Do not lie, bear false witness, use harsh, hateful, or divisive language, gossip, be rude, engage in useless chatter, etc. Always speak truthfully and lovingly in a manner that brings joy, hope, and understanding to others. Our speech should be guided by right view and right thinking.

4. Right Action or Conduct.

Engage in moral, ethical, honorable, and peaceful action. Practice nonviolence and be committed to protecting all life on earth.

5. Right Livelihood.

Choose a profession that is honorable, ethical, and helps and sustains living things rather than one that supports war, killing, disharmony, or harms, cheats, or exploits them. Five types of livelihoods to be avoided are specifically mentioned:

- Trade in any kind of weapons.
- Any form of trade in human beings.
- Breeding and selling of animals for slaughter.

- Manufacture or sale of addictive drugs or intoxicating drinks.
- Production or trade of any kind of toxic substance or poison designed to harm living things.

6. Right Effort or Diligence. (Paraphrased from Rahula referenced below)

Right diligence is a concerted effort (1) to prevent evil and unwholesome states of mind from arising, (2) to rid one's self from such thoughts that have already arisen (3) to produce good and wholesome states of mind that have not yet arisen, and (4) to develop and bring to perfection the good and wholesome states of mind already present.

7. Right Mindfulness.

Right mindfulness is being diligently aware of activities of the body, our sensations and feelings, and our thoughts (and their nature). It is being mindful of and living in the present moment free from all thoughts or concern about the past or the future. In mindfulness we refrain from judgement or interpretation of what we are experiencing in the moment. When we are mindful, right thinking, right speech, right action, etc. will be expressed.

8. Right Concentration.

Buddha said that when we have a singleness of mind supported by the other seven factors of the Noble Eightfold

Path we have achieved right concentration. It is an essential component of effective meditation.

Right concentration is described as a one-pointed mind. That is, the ability to focus or concentrate on one thing. Right concentration encompasses and is facilitated and supported by the other seven elements of the Noble Path. The practice of right concentration allows us to cultivate insight and develop wisdom by examination of the true nature of things through meditation.

It is by striving to follow the Noble Eightfold Path in our everyday life that we develop the basic principles of ethical conduct, mental discipline, and wisdom which are central to Buddhist practice. Buddha gave many discourses on each element of the Path to explain their meaning in great depth. Consequently, my brief explanations are sorely incomplete and do not give a full appreciation of the scope and quality of each element of the Path.

While many components of the Eightfold Path are things for which most people seeking a spiritual way of life would strive, the Path codifies a stepwise process to achieve them. The Noble Eightfold Path encompasses universal elements of a spiritual way of life. Many of them resonate with the teachings of Christianity and other religions.

I would place persons who engage in spiritual practices and thought akin to those of Buddhists among the exalted meek that are said to one day inherit the earth. In a world seemingly filled with murky shadows and darkness, they are a beacon of light and hope.

References

Hanh, Thich Nhat, *The Heart of the Buddha's Teaching. Transforming Suffering into Peace, Joy, and Liberation.* New York: Harmony Books. 2010. First published 1999.

Rahula, Walpola. *What the Buddha Taught. 2nd ed. enlarg. New York: Grove Press. 1974.* First published 1959.

March 6, 2016

A Letter to God

Dear God,

I am writing to ask that through your grace and the efforts of your Holy Spirits that the dark minds of the wicked and selfish be turned toward the light of goodness, love, and compassion. I ask that you give us world leaders and governments that are driven by a strong desire for the happiness, health, and wellbeing of their people and by a strong desire for a peaceful world.

I realize that transformation is a very slow process and that sometimes it is only through great suffering that change takes place; that sometimes it is only through great injustice that justice can finally be achieved; that sometimes it is only through darkness that the search for light and truth begins.

It appears that you have set into motion circumstances to motivate us to change as individuals and as a civilization.

You have pointed the way, but I understand that it is up to each of us to contribute to the creation of a better world for ourselves.

I pray with all my heart that the majority of us will hear your call and respond to adversity, not with anger, aggression, or grasping, but rather with equanimity and a strong desire to help one another get through the trials and tribulations we face, and to find lasting happiness through continuing acts of love and compassion.

I am and forever will be your devoted servant.

May 7, 2016

How is My Divine Self Revealed?

If I am a child of God, then what is the essence of my divine nature? How is my divine self revealed?

I believe that the divine self is manifested by the spirit and that love and compassion are spiritual attributes. Therefore, one way in which we reveal our divinity is by expression of love and compassion for all things.

Compassion is not an attribute exclusive to people of religious faith. In fact, it did not originate in religion; rather, it is an aspect of our in-born divine nature. It is an attribute of *humanity*. Everyone has it, but we often get lost from time to time on our life path and stray from our inherent loving and generous nature. What is important is that we recognize that the spiritual gifts of love and compassion are at the core of our being; that when we express these qualities, we are revealing our divinity to ourselves and to those whose lives we touch.

Nothing is more rewarding or more important in life than sharing these spiritual gifts with others. What is important in the pursuit of meaning in our lives is that we all aspire and strive to express our divinity in various ways on a daily basis. It is through these actions that our divine self is revealed.

May 25, 2016

So You Say You Are Spiritual...

If you have chosen to move away from organized religion or you were not brought up in a home where religion was a part of life, you are not a spiritual person simply by default. When asked about your religious affiliation, replying that you are "spiritual" does not make it so. Neither does viewing yourself as such.

In order to truly be spiritual, a few things are needed from you. First, you need to be aware that you have a spirit; that your spirit is what gives life to you. It is behind your life force and it can guide and influence your thoughts and actions if you let it.

Having made this realization, then one is usually compelled to explore and understand the fundamental nature of spirituality. This is essential because being spiritual is a way of living and a way of viewing the universe, the world, our place in them, and the meaning of life. Spirituality can arise and thrive within or without structured religion.

Once you come to truly understand that you are a spiritual being, everything changes. One of the changes is that you move away from the material aspects of life to the non-material qualities of existence. Your focus shifts away from things and self-serving behaviors and thoughts to unselfish concern for the wellbeing of all living things. This is a major paradigm shift in world view for most people, especially in the years leading up to midlife.

Once one acknowledges the presence of their spirit-self, the journey to discover what it means to be spiritual and to live the life of spirit begins. My hope and prayer is that it will come early in life for as many as possible.

June 16, 2016

Just So...

What is this heavenly radiance I see before me with such uncanny beauty?

It's like a sky full of stars, but it is morning.

The light emitted is bright, beautiful, wondrous, and other worldly, so much so that I find myself trying to catch my breath.

I cannot take my eyes off the dazzling display

Of what looks to be sparkling diamonds

And precious gems of all kinds

With fire like I have never seen before.

Hundreds of water droplets clinging to a screen

Have caught the early morning light, just so...

Resulting in refraction of the light, just so...

Each droplet sparkles and pulsates with its own unique color.

The panoply of colors can be seen in all shades and hues

That is more vivid and vibrant than I could have ever imagined.

Is this how the universe of stars would look, if the dust and light years between us were removed?

Or is this the quality of light seen in the heavenly realms?

But alas, the gentle morning sunbeams that gave light, just so...

Impinging on ordinary droplets of water at an angle, just so...

Giving birth to such incredible beauty...

Must now give way to a rising sun

And I am quickly transported back to earth.

Exhilarated by what I have just seen,

I realize that there is so much more

That is beyond our ordinary perception.

There is another world of unimaginable wonders.

A revelation that was given, just so...

June 17, 2016

Sentinels of Peace

I have been feeling the need to get out among a forest of trees. Nature and wilderness have been calling to me for some time now.

When I visited my daughter in Colorado last year, we went up to Lookout Mountain. What I really liked most about it was sitting under the trees while eating our lunch. It felt so welcoming and comforting. I could have sat there for hours and just listen to the breeze in the branches.

It was like a homecoming and having the love of family all around you. With all of the branches overhead and the tree trunks all around, I felt safe and protected. I had found sanctuary and tranquility. When it was time to go my spirit protested, reluctant to leave a place of such beauty, serenity, and unconditional love.

Now the forest land beckons me once again. My heart yearns for reunion with my stalwart sentinels of peace.

June 28, 2016

An Expression of the Spirit

My dear God,

I ask for your guidance, and the strength, determination, and courage to serve you to the best of my ability, at all times, without fail, in any manner you ask of me, without hesitation or fear.

My only desire is to serve and honor you by expression of my spirit through continual acts of love, compassion, and healing.

This is my heart's desire. This is who I wish to be.

This is who I am.

This is who I have always been and always will be.

July 10, 2016

Spirit's Answer to My Prayer

Love and compassion are not mental processes; rather, they are an expression of the spirit. Follow your heart and let them flow freely without thought, fear, or any other product of the mind. Do what comes naturally and have faith that you are being guided. Be of the conviction that the actions to help others compelled by the expression of love and compassion (of the spirit) always will be healing and nurturing to the soul of the recipient.

July 23, 2016

An Echo in the Woods

I hear a distant voice calling.
Like an echo in the woods.

I pay no attention
But it keeps coming back
Like a poem's refrain.

It's telling me there is *more...*
More than what I see all around me.

More to be done than simply satisfy my selfish needs.
It's telling me that I am so much more than this body.
That I am so much more than my puny mind allows me to believe.

The voice is telling me that I have infinite potential
And great power as yet untapped.

It calls me to a more noble and meaningful existence.

An echo in the woods...

Do you hear it?

August 3, 2016

A Path from Darkness

...and Spirit told me, "Do not be consumed with fear and regret for past sins. Your transgressions should be neither dismissed nor forgotten. Rather, recognize them as lessons to be learned and do not repeat them. Use them to move forward and fuel your resolve to rise to higher levels of spiritual understanding and virtue."

September 17, 2016

The Scientific Aesthetic

If we were having coffee together, I would tell you how I wanted to be a scientist since about the age of ten or eleven. Unlike most children who declare a vocation at such a young age, I never lost sight of the goal and did indeed become a scientist (now retired).

But the other day I was thinking about what it was that kept my dream alive from childhood to fruition as an adult. I mean how many young kids who say they want to be a fireman actually becomes one? What I realized was that I had an abiding wonder and fascination with all of the mysteries of nature. Science was a tool to reveal its secrets.

As a young boy, I wanted to explore many and varied aspects of the natural world and science. For a time I was an avid mineralogist. I made many expeditions into the creek bed behind the apartments where I lived. My holy grail was to find a geode; I never found one but found some petrified wood instead. I was disappointed at the time, but years later realized how cool and unusual that find was.

I had an inexpensive microscope and peered into the previously unseen details of all sorts of things from hair to bugs and leaves. When the Russians launched Sputnik in 1957, the first satellite, I became fascinated with rockets and space travel. Yes...of course, I fabricated my own rocket. It was a unique home design made from an aluminum pipe with balsa wood tail fins and a crude fuel made with chemicals in my chemistry set. Back then the sets included the components needed to make gun powder—oops.

I realized in retrospect that my design was badly flawed—more like a dangerous firework than a rocket— but it did manage a few flights of maybe 50 feet up before the aluminum could no longer withstand the blast. Thank God my brother and I had the good sense to run like hell when the fuse was lit!
As time went on, I began to develop a pantheistic view of the world. My vision moved beyond practical, objective aspects of my surroundings to an aesthetic appreciation.

Into middle age, my relationship with science and nature became more inspirational and spiritual, and less investigative. Rather than study and analyze nature, I wanted to experience it. Rather than simply being a refuge from daily life, the natural world became a celebration of the diversity of life—something sacred to be revered, loved, and protected.

Thus, I have come full circle; once again I have that innocent sense of wonder and I am amazed and thrilled by the incredible beauty and complexity of the natural world around me, just as I was as a young boy growing up.

October 22, 2016

Spirits Calling

Upon leaving the gym today I was compelled to stop by a small grove of trees that was outside the entrance. As I looked up into the branches with flashes of the sun passing through on the breeze, I felt so much love. Love *for* the beautiful trees and love *from* the trees.

They could just as well have been angels of God. It was a remarkably sublime feeling of calm, contentment, and fulfillment. It was a wonderful spiritual moment.

I have walked past those trees hundreds of times without noticing them. But this day I heard them call to me and say, "Come, stay a while and let us commune with God and feel His love."

October 11, 2017

How Does One Sustain a Spiritual Outlook?

A friend recently asked me, "How does one sustain their spirituality?" The answer to that question will be somewhat different for each person. Some may say that participation in religious practice and/or community is needed to sustain one's spirituality. Those things can have role, but what we're addressing here is a continuity of spirituality throughout everyday of our lives.

For me, spirituality is not only a way of living, but also a state of mind. It is that state of mind or spiritual presence that is the key to sustaining one's spirituality. In some ways it is like being in a constant state of prayer or contact with God and the spiritual realm.

As we move through our day, we should always be silently expressing our gratitude and thanks for every little thing we

see, experience, and receive. We should strive to always be present and to take notice of the many expressions and beauty of God all around us. We should allow feelings of love and compassion to come forth naturally, unfiltered by the intellect or prejudice.

When we do these things, we allow our spirit to express and commune with God and His holy spirits. Then we find ourselves in a constant state of grace, happiness, contentment, and bliss.

October 15, 2018

I Had a Vision...

I had a vision of what someday will be. I saw a wave of love, compassion, and healing emanating from God spread around the world leaving the earth enveloped in a soft glow of divine energy. Peace and tranquility permeated the awareness of all living things. The rotation of the earth seemed to quicken with excitement, just for a moment.

It was a vision of a world in perfect harmony. There was no more suffering. People treated each other with dignity, respect, generosity, and kindness. No one was left cold, hungry, or without shelter.

The planet was vibrant and healthy. The air was clean, fresh, and fragrant. The animals came out in the warm sunlight to play, unafraid.

I am confident that one day these things will come to pass; such is the destiny of humanity and planet Earth. Each of us must do all that we can, here and now, to make that vision a reality. Each of us through our actions, attitudes, and the example we provide can begin to bring about change in the small slice of the world in which we live. Our individual efforts will have a local additive effect which over time will spread geographically and eventually exponentially.

The Gift of Presence

Being present in the moment is a big thing these days, as it should be. It is something with which I struggle on a daily basis. Intellectually we can appreciate the value of being present, but putting it into practice is difficult; old habits of the mind are hard to change. And what can we expect should we achieve the holy grail of Presence anyway?

But then I recently had a remarkable experience that gave me a taste of just how wonderful and transforming complete, unwavering presence can be. As I walked out of a movie theater I inexplicably stopped dead in my tacks. There before me was the most mundane and superficially insipid scene you could imagine. I was looking out across a large parking lot...but somehow it was so much more than that at this particular moment.

I became totally immersed in the clouds along the horizon and the tall royal palm trees lining the street. The golden hour was approaching making the green and grey of the trees glow with a seemingly heavenly light. I studied the

113

shapes of the clouds and the lines of the tree trunks. My eyes were transfixed on the scene. I felt a deep appreciation and affection for each element of the scene—the trees, the sky, and clouds. I felt exceedingly alive and happy. So much so that I stood there for quite some time scanning the scene. I didn't want to take even one step and lose these feelings of joy.

As I drove home, my mind continued to seek presence in what I saw along the way, but sadly I was forced to keep my eyes on the road and attend to my driving. I had hoped that I would re-enter the mystical state of awareness I had experienced when I got home but it was not to be—not then, the next day, or the days to follow. I was left disappointed and wondering just what it was that I experienced and how to get back there again.

During that short span of presence I saw the beauty and wonder of simple things around me in great detail. What usually was a mind busy with useless thoughts was totally focused on what was before me. It showed me that when we are truly present in the moment, we see things we didn't notice before. We see the beauty in things that previously scarcely caught our attention.

When present and interacting with others, we perceive beyond the superficiality of appearance and words. As Thich Nhat Hanh has suggested, we hear and see people deeply with greater understanding and compassion.

Achieving presence is well worth the effort because it can lead to an elevated state of being and awareness which in turn will lead to greater happiness and joy. The simplest things can be seen as they really are: beautiful and fascinating. This is the gift of presence.

April 19, 2018

The Trilogy of Harmony

Those interested in spirituality—what it is and how to become a spiritual person—sooner or later come across the notion of harmony between spirit, mind, and body. What exactly does it mean and how do you get there? To get there one has to cultivate each of its three aspects of being. Achievement of this Trilogy of Harmony leads to sustained peace, joy, and equanimity.

A healthy, physically fit body is one of the pillars of attaining harmony between spirit, mind, and body. As an example, if we don't feel well, or we're weak, frail, or sick, it is difficult to think clearly. Likely we are concerned about our health which takes a toll on our mind.

Furthermore, ills of the body often reflect an imbalance in the spirit. We may be unable to experience lasting joy and happiness. Our worries, guilt, and regret prevent us from finding peace and equanimity.

Mental products such as our attitudes, behaviors, thoughts, and actions can either feed and elevate the spirit or damage and debilitate it. This is governed by the Law of Cause and Effect. The health of our spirit is determined in large part by the way we treat other people. One should always strive to live a life characterized by honesty, integrity, compasssion, and ethical behavior.

We can cultivate the mind by meditation, striving to be wholly present through mindfulness and working to stop the constant train of useless thoughts so many of us experience. It is also important to allow only wholesome thoughts, and to maintain a positive and virtuous outlook.

A cultivated mind and body naturally leads to a greater expression of our spirit in everyday life. Buddha's Four Immeasurables well illustrate the essence of spiritual expression and the results of the Trilogy of Harmony.

The Immeasurables are: love, compassion, equanimity, and empathetic joy. These four are also known as the four sublime or extraordinary states of mind, which to me, illustrate the affect the spirit can have on the mind.

I hope from this discussion you begin to see the importance of achieving the Trilogy of Harmony for a happy, healthy, rewarding, and productive life, and how the spirit, mind, and body support and interact with each other. If any one of these three pillars of harmony is not in a healthy, positive state, then the trilogy is broken. As we all know, each of the three components can function independently, but without the elevated state of being (especially of the spirit) that the Trilogy of Harmony brings. You cannot give yourself a gift greater than the fulfillment, happiness, joy, and peace that achieving this harmony will create.

May 28, 2018

The Divine Virtues

A mind that is free, open, and present is the key to achieving harmony between spirit, mind, and body. The mind is the intermediary between the spirit and the body. It is the essential link needed in order for qualities of the spirit to be manifested in the physical world through emotions and actions. By spiritual qualities I mean things like love, compassion, forgiveness, and healing energy. These are the divine virtues that all human spirits have.

Free expression of the divine virtues is characteristic of a truly spiritual life. The mind must make the decision to put

aside any fears, insecurities, or prejudice and let the divine virtues flow naturally to everyone we encounter in our everyday lives without favoritism.

September 9, 2018

How Life Works

The short answer is that how our lives unfold depends on our outlook, motivations, intentions, and how we treat others. The effect of these factors on the quality and prevailing course of a person's life is governed by two interrelated natural or spiritual laws.

The Law of Cause and Effect

This law embodies the biblical saying "You reap what you sow." It is also related to the popular concept of karma which says that we create our own futures (in this life or the next) by our actions and how we treat others. If we do not stop our wrongdoing and change how we live our lives for the better, then we can expect an ongoing chain of negative effects on us and those around us. However, cause and effect provides the opportunity to break free from past bad behaviors and attitudes, and change our future.

Even as our karma plays out, we can decide what direction our life will take. Will we choose a fulfilling and happy life of goodness, love, and compassion, or a life of bitterness, jealousy, selfishness, greed, and hate devoid of any redeeming factors? Will we surrender to the darkness we have brought upon ourselves, or will we refuse to give up and instead emerge from the muck and blaze a new path toward spiritual awareness?

118

The Law of Compensation and Retribution

The Law of Compensation and Retribution is inherent in, and a natural consequence of, the Law of Cause and Effect. You will be rewarded for striving to live a life of goodness, and for helping others any way you can. Unselfish acts of loving kindness can compensate for past wrongdoing and transgressions of spiritual laws. However, wrongdoing in the absence of compensatory acts will result in retribution that leads to a life of suffering, unhappiness, and regret.

Thus, through free will and cause and effect, each of us determines the course of our own lives. *The outcome cannot be attributed to anyone or anything other than ourselves.*

This is a critical principle of spiritual law that once understood makes it possible for us to find true happiness and fulfillment. It means that we have the power to change our lives for the better and through our love and compassion the lives of others. It provides the opportunity to progress spiritually and fulfill our purpose in this life on Earth.

The laws of cause and effect and compensation and retribution, like the Law of Gravity, once set into motion by our creator require no ongoing oversight. The spiritual laws operate automatically and assure accountability and justice concerning all of our thoughts and actions. I hope that everyone can appreciate what a simple and perfect plan this is. We get exactly what we deserve in terms of punishment or reward. It is the ultimate learning tool.

The natural or spiritual laws discussed here can be found in various books in the Silver Birch series (e.g., *The Teachings of Silver Birch*).

October 14, 2018

One God, One People

One people: with a singular origin.

All related by birth

One family: its members' interconnections

Inextricable.

Be not estranged from your kin.

Embrace the interdependence among all people.

Look fondly upon all of your brothers and sisters.

Help those in need.

Show them kindness and compassion.

Express your inherited divinity!

August 1, 2019

Daily Prayer for Healing

My dear God,

I pray for mercy and healing for everyone who suffers. May the healing we receive give us the strength to endure, overcome, and transcend our pain and suffering, and where appropriate, our circumstances.

And may it lift our sprints and strengthen our hope and faith in a better future, not just for ourselves, but for all of humanity.

My Lord, I love you with all my heart, mind, soul, spirit, and strength.

I am, and forever will be, your devoted servant.
Amen

November 2, 2019

The Coming of a New Day

...And Spirit said: All of the pain, suffering, social turmoil, and destruction happening around the world herald the coming of a new day. It is leading humanity toward greater humility, nobility, compassion, and virtue. Be strong, but do not resist your transformation!

June 22, 2020

The Essence of Spirituality

Ultimately, spirituality is about people and how they interact with one another.

Like art, spirituality is a personal expression of beauty, emotion, and soul.

July 9, 2020

The Pillars of Spirituality

It seems likely that most people would consider love and compassion as universal qualities of a spiritual person. At the same time, study of the life of prominent spiritual figures such as Jesus and Buddha demonstrate other important attributes of a spiritual being.

The Four Immeasurables, also known as the Four Perfect Virtues, or as I prefer to call them, the Divine Virtues, are part of a more expansive integrated and intertwined spiritual wholeness. In my view, they are the four pillars of spirituality. The Divine Virtues can be seen as composing the "body" of the spirit. They are "internal organs" of the spirit. They keep it healthy, alive, and functioning the way it is intended.

The Divine Virtues of love, compassion, empathetic joy, and equanimity interact with, and inform one another. They are mutually *inclusive*. There is no need to reconcile one with the other; they all comprise a single being and a singular *way* of being.

Our personal joy and happiness arise naturally from practice of the Divine Virtues. Empathetic joy refers to joy in us arising from witnessing the special talents, successes, and good fortune of others. Empathetic joy radiates our love for the person being observed, and our gratitude for their God-given gifts.

Equanimity is mental calm, composure, and even-temper in all situations. In the context of spirituality, it is a state of inner peace from which we are able to view the world objectively, without prejudice, judgement, or emotional reaction. It is a place from which love and compassion radiate.

The inner peace that fosters equanimity can be achieved through meditation, prayer, and for some, through Chinese internal energy arts such as qigong which incorporate mindfulness into the practice. All of these serve to calm and nurture the spirit, mind, and body.

Love and compassion go hand-in-hand and lead to joy and happiness. There can be no compassion if the element of love is missing and vice versa.

How can one have empathetic joy for the happiness and special gifts we see in others without love? How can one have love, compassion, or joy in the midst of one's own anger, hate, jealousy, greed, fear, or emotional reaction to difficult situations?

Through equanimity, we can control our emotions and reactions so that we can clearly and objectively hear and see what is before us, and seek understanding and appreciation through patience, love, and compassion. Equanimity provides the peaceful environment, within which the other three Divine Virtues can thrive, grow, and radiate.

December 27, 2020

Compassion as Healing

...And when he came into the garden, he saw the boy sitting with his face in his hands, weeping. He asked, "Why are you crying?"

The boy replied, "When I think about all of the suffering around the world, it's painful and overwhelming. I feel powerless to help."

"But you are helping; your compassion has *power*. Acknowledging the suffering of others allows us to radiate healing energy. It also gets the attention of those in the spirit realm who have the ability to bring healing to the earth plane."

Hearing this, the boy said, "If what you say is true, then compassion may be the universal remedy for suffering of all kinds! How can the solution be so simple?"

"As I said, compassion has power. It starts a stream of healing energy and motivates people to seek ways to help the afflicted. The help we extend to those in need is healing not just to them, but also to *us.*"

With that the boy wiped away his tears, gave his mentor a big hug of gratitude, and went away smiling.

June 12, 2021

Step One

Genuine, heart-felt compassion is step one for becoming a spiritual person. We cannot claim to be spiritual in any way without it.

Once we take that step and consistently look outward (as well as inward), we will have set out on a path to greater spiritual awareness.

Compassion is a powerful, unspoken prayer for mercy and healing for those who suffer.

June 26, 2021

A Statement of Faith

Perhaps we all wonder at one time or another why there is so much pain and suffering? Why is life so difficult at times? Why do "bad" things happen to good people? And many other perplexing questions.

We have to accept that there are some things that we are not meant to know or that our current level of spiritual awareness precludes understanding. I believe in the old adage:" everything happens for a reason." This is a statement of faith in spiritual processes aimed at fostering our spiritual development.

It's important to remember that understanding what is beneficial or harmful to our spiritual development requires a view from the perspective of eternity to which we are not privy. Something thought to be "bad" now, may in fact, be good for our development in the flow of eternity. After all, we tend to become stronger, more spiritually enlightened, and to learn lessons best from adversity.

October 2, 2021

The Key to Effective Prayer

Prayer will be heard with greatest effect when it comes spontaneously from the heart and soul expressing in your own words your desire to help others or to become a more spiritual person.

Do not pray for material things because God has already provided what you need. Do not pray for elevation of your earthly status, for it counts for nothing in the spiritual realm. Rather, pray for elevation of your soul through expression of love, compassion, and service.

You might like to see the discussion of prayer that appears on pages 76-81 in *The Teachings of Silver Birch,* edited by A.W. Austin.

October 31, 2021

Religion and Spirituality

In my view, spirituality and religion are related, but not the same thing. Religion has arisen in an attempt to codify spiritual thought and ideas by the establishment of dogma, creeds, stories, and other traditions and to make it "experiential" through ritual and repetitive prayers.

But these things can distract us from the organic spirituality present in all of us. They can distract us from the spontaneous human experience of our spiritual nature and longing.

December 29, 2021

An Expanded Faith

It's important to have faith...in God, yes...but more generally, faith in the spiritual forces and challenges that shape our lives in ways that lead us to greater love, compassion, and spiritual awareness.

January 23, 2022

The Karma of Thoughts

The forces of cause and effect operate not only in response to behaviors, things we do or do not do, but also to the nature of our thoughts. If our thoughts are filled with love and compassion, then good things will come to us. If our minds are filled with anger, hate, or malice, then we will not have happiness and fulfillment, and spiritual retribution is sure to come.

March 13, 2022

Earth Karma

Cause and effect does not only apply to our interactions and treatment of people. It also applies to our actions concerning the natural environment and the planet as a whole.

As citizens of Earth, we have an obligation to not only care for one another, but also for all living things. We should view ourselves as stewards of the earth, all of its inhabitants, and its physical and ecological environs.

We will be held accountable for our actions that result in, or contribute to, the destruction of habitats, extinction of animal and plant species, pollution, and climate change. Retribution for our past abuses of the planet has already begun.

July 7, 2022

When Death Comes to Call

Fear not when death comes to call...

It will take you to another world

Free from the burden of the body.

A place of indescribable beauty,

That has infinite possibilities and profound opportunity.

Fear not, for you will be delivered into loving hands.

Epilogue

Heavenly Father,

I pledge to do my best to live every day in accord with what is written here. I pray that the words will transform me into a more kind, loving, compassionate, and generous human being. I now understand what it means to be a truly spiritual person. I will strive to exemplify those character-istics every day of my life.

Amen

Afterword

I entered into the spiritual blogosphere as a means by which to process and record my developing understanding of what it means to be a spiritual person at the most fundamental level. The goal was to sift through the spiritual wisdom of a diverse group of world religions to identify a common core of spiritual values and behaviors.

I found that love, compassion, and service to others are primary, minimum essential attributes needed to be a genuine spiritual person. Although we often equate spirituality with religion, religious beliefs are in no way requisite for living a vital and rewarding spiritual life. In fact, one could argue that religious dogma and practice can divert attention away from the more organic and natural aspects of spiritual life.

Author's Books and Blog Sites

Books

Atherton, Blair T. *Building a Bridge Between Two Worlds. Living the Life of Spirit.* Coral Springs, FL: Temple Thomas Publishing, 2012

Atherton, Blair T. *An Echo in the Woods. The Revelation of More.* Coral Springs, FL: Temple Thomas Publishing, *2017*

Atherton, Blair T. *The Golden Light of a Spiritual Dawn.* Coral Springs, FL: Temple Thomas Publishing, *2022*

Blog Sites

Exploring Spirituality Beyond Religion
www.livingthelifeofspirit.com

Spiritual Adventures. Contact with the Ether
www.needforhealing.org